THE DRESSER

RONALD HARWOOD

THE DRESSER

GROVE PRESS, INC., NEW YORK

First published in 1980 by Amber Lane Press, England.

First Evergreen Edition 1981
First Printing 1981
ISBN: 0-394-17936-6
Library of Congress Catalog Card Number: 81-47637

Library of Congress Cataloging in Publication Data

Harwood, Ronald, 1934–
    The dresser.

    I. Title.
PR6058.A73D7   1981   822'.914   81-13244
ISBN 0-394-17936-6 (pbk.)   AACR2

Manufactured in the United States of America

GROVE PRESS, INC., 196 West Houston Street, New York, N.Y. 10014

For my children,
Antony, Deborah and
Alexandra Harwood

Foreword

Because I was Sir Donald Wolfit's dresser for almost five years, it may be thought that the actor-manager in my play is a portrait of Wolfit, and that his relationship with his dresser is a dramatised account of our relationship. There may be other reasons for such a supposition: Lear was Wolfit's greatest performance—so is it Sir's; the grand manner both on and off the stage which Wolfit often employed is also Sir's way; the war did not stop Wolfit from playing Shakespeare in the principal provincial cities and in London; Sir is on tour in 1941, though playing less important dates. But there the similarities, and others less important, all wholly deliberate on my part, end. Sir is not Donald Wolfit. My biography* of the actor, with all its imperfections, must serve to reflect my understanding of him as a man and as a theatrical creature.

There is no denying, however, that my memory of what took place night after night in Wolfit's dressing room is part of the inspiration of the play. I witnessed at close quarters a great actor preparing for a dozen or more major classical roles which included Oedipus, Lear, Macbeth and Volpone. I was an observer also of the day-to-day responsibilities which management demanded and, later, as Wolfit's business-manager, partook of those responsibilities. I was a member of the crew who created the storm in *King Lear* which, however tempestuous, was never loud enough for Wolfit, as it never is for Sir. These and other countless memories undeniably fed my imaginings while writing the play.

Sources of another kind were of equal importance. I was fortunate, when young, to meet Sir John Martin-Harvey's stage manager; I held two long conversations with Charles Doran, the actor-manager who gave Wolfit his first job; I shared a dressing-room with an old actor, Malcolm Watson, who walked on in Sir Henry Irving's production of *Beckett* at the Lyceum; I worked with several old Bensonians—members of Sir Frank Benson's Shakespearean Company—and I knew Robert Atkins who, for many years, ran the seasons at the Open Air Theatre, Regent's Park. A number of the actors Wolfit employed were what used to be called 'Shakespeareans', men and women who had played with Alexander Marsh, Henry Bainton, H. J. Saintsbury and other actor-managers not of the front rank. There was, too, in Wolfit's company, a wonderfully robust actor called Frank G. Cariello whose greatest professional disappointment was that Martin-Harvey, after allowing him to play Laertes on tour, re-cast the part for London. Cariello, himself briefly an actor-manager, was a tireless and witty raconteur with a prodigious memory of theatrical times past. The atmosphere engendered by these men, imbibed by me before I was 20, was much in my mind when writing the play.

The tradition of actor-management made a deep impression on me. I came to understand that from the early 18th century until the late 1930s the actor-manager was the British theatre. He played from one end of the country to the other, taking his repertoire to the people. Only a handful ever reached London; their stamping-ground was the provinces and they toured under awful physical conditions, undertaking long, uncomfortable railway journeys on Sundays, spending many hours waiting for their connections in the cold at Crewe. They developed profound resources of strength, essential if they were to survive. They worshipped Shakespeare, believed in the theatre as a cultural and educative force, and saw themselves as public servants. Nowadays, we allow ourselves to laugh at them a little and there is no denying that their obsessions and single-mindedness often made them ridiculous; we are inclined to write them off as megalomaniacs and hams; we accept, too readily I think, that their motto was *'le théâtre c'est moi!'* The truth of the matter is that many of them were extraordinary and talented men; their gifts enhanced the art of acting; they nursed and kept alive a classical repertoire which is the envy of the world, and created a magnificent tradition which is the foundation of our present-day theatrical inheritance.

I must acknowledge also words written by and about them: Sir John Martin-Harvey's excellent autobiography from which I have quoted in the play, the works of James Agate, the biography of Irving by Laurence Irving and J. C. Trewin's splendid book, *The Theatre Since 1900.*

The play, however, is called *The Dresser.* No actor-manager ever survived entirely through his own efforts. Publicly he liked to proclaim pride in his individuality while acknowledging, in private, his debt to all those who devoted their lives to him and to his enterprise. The character of Norman is in no way autobiographical. He, like Sir, is an amalgam of three or four men I met who served leading actors as professional dressers. Norman's relationship with Sir is not mine with Wolfit. No other character in the play is wholly based on a real person. Her Ladyship is quite unlike Rosalind Iden (Lady Wolfit). I have considered it necessary to make these disclaimers in order to give a truer background to the play. I know to my cost that once a mistaken interpretation attaches to a work of imagination it is difficult, if not impossible, to dispel.

Ronald Harwood

*Sir Donald Wolfit, C.B.E. His life and work in the unfashionable theatre. (London: Secker & Warburg, 1971)

The Dresser was first performed at the Royal Exchange Theatre, Manchester on 6 March 1980 with the following cast:

NORMAN	Tom Courtenay
HER LADYSHIP	Isabel Dean
IRENE	Jacqueline Tong
MADGE	Carole Gillies
SIR	Freddie Jones
GEOFFREY THORNTON	Lockwood West
MR OXENBY	Geoffrey McGivern

Players in *King Lear*

Gloucester	Rex Arundel
Knight Albany }	Anthony Benson
Knight Gentleman }	Joe Holmes
Kent	Guy Nicholls

Directed by Michael Elliott
Set designed by Laurie Dennett
Costumes designed by Stephen Doncaster
Lighting by Mark Henderson
Sound by Ian Gibson

The play was presented at the Queen's Theatre, London on 30 April 1980 by Michael Codron with the following change of cast:

HER LADYSHIP	Jane Wenham
MADGE	Janet Henfrey
Knight Gentleman }	Peter O'Dwyer
Knight Albany }	Kenneth Oxtoby
Kent	David Browning
Electrician	Trevor Griffiths

Characters

NORMAN
HER LADYSHIP
MADGE
SIR
IRENE
GEOFFREY THORNTON
MR OXENBY
Two Knights, Gloucester, Kent.

January 1942. A theatre in the English provinces.

Act I: Before curtain-up.
Act II: After curtain-up.

ACT ONE

SIR's *dressing room and corridor. Light on* NORMAN, *who wears a lost, almost forlorn expression. Light grows to reveal a mud-stained overcoat and crumpled Homburg lying on the floor. Footsteps.* NORMAN *becomes alert. He rises.* HER LADYSHIP *enters. She stands just inside the doorway.*

HER LADYSHIP:	He does nothing but cry.
NORMAN:	Are they keeping him in?
HER LADYSHIP:	They wouldn't let me stay. The doctor said I seemed to make matters worse.
NORMAN:	I shouldn't have taken him to the hospital. I don't know what came over me. I should have brought him back here where he belongs.
HER LADYSHIP:	Why is his coat on the floor? And his hat—?
NORMAN:	Drying out. They're wet through, sodden, if you don't mind my saying so. So was he. Drenched. Sweat and drizzle—
HER LADYSHIP:	How did he come to be in such a state, Norman? When you telephoned, I thought at first he'd been hurt in the air raid—
NORMAN:	No—
HER LADYSHIP:	Or had an accident—
NORMAN:	No, not an accident—
HER LADYSHIP:	No, I know because they said there was no sign of physical injury—
NORMAN:	Your ladyship—
HER LADYSHIP:	He's in a state of collapse—
NORMAN:	I know—
HER LADYSHIP:	How did he get like that?
NORMAN:	Your ladyship—

HER LADYSHIP: What happened to him?

NORMAN: Sit down. Please. Please, sit down.

[*She does so.*]

We have to remain calm, not to say clear-headed.

HER LADYSHIP: The doctor said it must have been coming on for weeks.

NORMAN: If not longer.

HER LADYSHIP: I didn't see him this morning. He left the digs before I woke. Where was he all day? Where did you find him?

NORMAN: What happened was this, your ladyship: after the last 'All-clear' sounded I went into Market Square as dusk was coming on, a peculiar light, ever so yellowish, smoke and dust rising from the bomb craters, running shadows, full of the unexpected. I had hoped to find a packet or two of Brown and Polson's cornflour since our supplies are rather low and the stuff's scarce and you never know. So I was asking at this stall and that when I heard his voice.

HER LADYSHIP: Whose voice?

NORMAN: Sir's, of course. I turned and saw him by the candle-maker who was shutting up shop for the night. He was lit by one tall tallow candle which was guttering and he looked like that painting of him as Lear, all greens and dark blues seen through this peculiar light. He was taking off his overcoat, in this weather. "God help the man who stops me," he shouted, and threw the coat to the ground just like Lear in the storm scene. Look at it. I don't know if I'll ever get it clean. And he was so proud of it, do you remember, or perhaps it was before your time? The first Canadian tour, Toronto, Raglan sleeves, fur collar, and now look at it.

HER LADYSHIP: What happened after he took off his coat?

NORMAN: Started on the hat, Dunn's, Piccadilly, only a year ago, down on the coat it went and he jumped on it, stamped on it, viciously stamped on his hat. You can see. He lifted both hands as he does to convey sterility into Goneril's womb and called out, "How much further do you want me to go?" His fingers were all of a fidget, undoing his jacket, loosening his collar and tie, tearing at the buttons of his shirt.

HER LADYSHIP: Were there many people about?

NORMAN: A small crowd. That's why I ran to him. I didn't want him to stand there looking ridiculous with people all round, sniggering.

HER LADYSHIP: Did he see you? Did he know who you were?

NORMAN: I didn't wait to find out. I just took his hand and said, "Good evening, Sir, shouldn't we be getting to the theatre?" in my best nanny-voice, the one I use when he's being way-ward. He paid no attention. He was shiver-ing. His whole body seemed to be trembling, and such a trembling.

HER LADYSHIP: You shouldn't have let the public see him like that.

NORMAN: It's easy to be wise after the event, if you don't mind my saying so, your ladyship, but I tried to spirit him away, not easy with a man of his proportions, only just then, a woman approached, quite old, wearing bombazine under a tweed coat but perfectly respectable. She'd picked up his clothes and wanted to help him dress. I just stood there, amazed, utterly amazed. He said to the woman, "Thank you my dear, but Norman usually looks after me. I'd be lost without Norman," so I thought to myself this is your cue, ducky, and said, "I'm Norman, I'm his dresser.'' The woman—she had her hair in curlers—took his hand and kissed it, saying, ''You were lovely in *The Corsican Brothers.''* He looked at her a long while, smiled sweetly, you know the way he does when he's wanting to charm, and said, ''Thank you, my dear, but you must excuse me. I have to make an exit,'' and ran off.

HER LADYSHIP: He said, I have to make an exit?

NORMAN: Well, of course, I went after him, fearing the worst. I didn't know he could run so fast. I just followed a trail of discarded clothing, jacket, waistcoat, and thought we can't have Sir doing a striptease round the town. But then I found him. Leaning up against a lamp-post. Weeping.

HER LADYSHIP: Where?

NORMAN: Outside the Kardomah. Without a word, hardly knowing what I was doing, I led him to the hospital. The Sister didn't recognise him, although later she said she'd seen him as Othello last night. A doctor was summoned, short, bald, bespectacled, and I was excluded by the drawing of screens.

HER LADYSHIP: And then you telephoned me.

NORMAN: No. I waited. I lurked, as Edmund says, and heard the doctor whisper, ''This man is exhausted. This man is in a state of collapse.'' Then the Sister came out and said I must fetch you at once. That's when I telephoned. And that's how it happened.

[*Pause. 'All-clear' sounds.*]

HER LADYSHIP: He did nothing but cry.

NORMAN: Yes, you said.

HER LADYSHIP: I left him lying on top of the bed, still in his clothes, crying, no, weeping, as though he had lost control, had no choice, wept and wept, floodgates. What are we to do? In just over an hour there'll be an audience in this theatre hoping to see him as King Lear. What am I to do?

NORMAN: Don't upset yourself for a start—

HER LADYSHIP: I've never had to make this sort of decision before. Any sort of decision before. As soon as I came out of the hospital I telephoned Madge and asked her to meet me here as soon as possible. She'll know what to do.

NORMAN: Oh yes, Madge will know what to do. She won't upset herself, that's for certain. Madge will be ever so sensible. Of course, Stage Managers have to be. I had a friend once, had been a vicar before falling from the pulpit and landing on the stage. Ever so good as an Ugly Sister. To the manner born. His wife didn't upset easily. Just as well, I suppose, all things considered. Madge reminds me of her. Cold, businesslike, boring.

[*Pause.*]

HER LADYSHIP: The doctor took me into a little room littered with enamel dishes full of blood-stained bandages. He apologised. They'd been busy after the air-raid. The smell made me faint. He asked me about his behaviour in recent days. Had I noticed anything untoward? I smiled. Involuntarily. Untoward. Such an odd word to use.

NORMAN: What did you say, if you don't mind my asking?

HER LADYSHIP: I lied. I said he'd been perfectly normal. I didn't want to appear neglectful. I should have been more vigilant. Only last night I woke—

[*Footsteps.* IRENE *enters the corridor.*]

Is that Madge?

NORMAN: No. Irene.

[IRENE *exits.*]

You were saying. Last night you woke.

HER LADYSHIP: He was looking down at me. He was naked. It was bitter cold and he was shivering. He said, "Thank you for watching over me. But don't worry too much. Just go on looking after me. I have the feeling I may do something violent."

NORMAN: Talk about untoward. I'm glad you didn't tell the doctor that, they'd have locked him up for good.

HER LADYSHIP: This morning, our landlady reported something untoward. After breakfast, while I was still asleep, he listened to the news, she said, and wept. Afterwards, he sat at the dining table writing, or trying to write, but all he did was to crumple up sheet after sheet of paper. When I came down I smoothed them out to see what he'd written. My Life. My Life. The rest of the page was empty.

NORMAN: He said to me his autobiography would be his only memorial. "Have you written much," I asked? "Not a word," he said. And last night, after Othello, he asked me, "What do we play tomorrow, Norman?" I told him *King Lear* and he said, "Then I shall wake with the storm clouds in my head."

HER LADYSHIP: I should have made him rest. The doctor said he'd come to the end of his rope and found it frayed.

NORMAN: So would anyone if they'd had to put up with what he's had to put up with. You should've told the doctor all about the troubles—

HER LADYSHIP: No. Civilians never understand.

NORMAN: That's true. Especially doctors. They never understand anything. I could kick myself for taking him to the hospital.

HER LADYSHIP: It was the right thing to do.

NORMAN: I hope so. Doctors. Just imagine trying to explain to a doctor what Sir's been through. "Well, you see, doctor, he's been trying to recruit actors for his Shakespearean company but all the able-bodied and best ones are in uniform, and the theatres are bombed to bits as soon as you book them, not to mention the trouble this week with Mr Davenport-Scott." Doctors. He'd have had his hypodermic rampant before you could say 'As You Like It'. That's all they know. Hypodermics. If a doctor had been through half of what Sir's been through, his rope wouldn't be frayed, it'd be threadbare.

HER LADYSHIP: What's the latest on Mr Davenport-Scott?

NORMAN: If you don't mind, I'd rather not discuss Mr Davenport-Scott with a lady. I'll tell Madge all about it when she comes in. Suffice to say he will not be making an appearance this evening. Of course, I told Sir. I said, "Don't, I beg you, don't let your business manager double as The Fool in *King Lear*." Now he's lost both in one fell blitzkrieg if you'll pardon the expression.
[*Pause.*]

HER LADYSHIP: Madge is right. There's no alternative. We'll have to cancel.

NORMAN: Oh no, your ladyship, cancellation's ever so drastic.

HER LADYSHIP: He's ill. There's no crime in being ill, it's not high treason, not a capital offence, not desertion in the face of the enemy. He's not himself. He can't work. Will the world stop turning? Will the Nazis overrun England? One Lear more or less in the world won't make any difference.

NORMAN: Sir always believes it will.

HER LADYSHIP: Who really cares whether he acts or not?

NORMAN: There's bound to be someone.

[*Pause.*]

HER LADYSHIP: I never imagined it would end like this. I've always thought he was indestructible. All the years we've been together. Seems like a lifetime.

NORMAN: Even longer he and I. This'll be the first time we've ever cancelled. I want to go to the hospital—

HER LADYSHIP: No, Norman—

NORMAN: I want to sit with him and be with him and try to give him comfort. I can usually make him smile. Perhaps when he sees me—

HER LADYSHIP: They wouldn't even let me stay.

[NORMAN *fights tears. Pause.*]

NORMAN: Sixteen years. I wish I could remember the name of the girl who got me into all this. Motherly type she was, small parts, play as cast. I can see her face clearly. I can see her standing there, Platform 2 at Crewe. A Sunday. I was on platform 4. "Norman" she called. We'd been together in *Outward Bound,* the Number Three tour, helped with wardrobe I did, understudied Scrubby, the steward. That's all aboard a ship, you know. Lovely first act. "We're all dead, aren't we?" And I say, "Yes, Sir, we're all dead. Quite dead." And he says, "How long have you been—you been—oh you know?" "Me, Sir? Oh, I was lost young." And he says, "Where—where are we sailing for?" And I say, "Heaven, Sir. And hell, too. It's the same place, you see." Lovely. Anyway. "Norman!" she called. What was her name? She'd joined Sir, oh, very hoity-toity, I thought, tiaras and blank verse while I was in panto understudying the Ugly Sisters.

Both of them. "Are you fixed?" she shouted
at the top of her voice. Well. To cut a short
story shorter, Sir wanted help in the wardrobe and someone to assist generally, but
mainly with the storm in *Lear*. I've told you
this before, haven't I? Put me on the timpani,
he did. On the first night, after the storm,
while he was waiting to go on for 'No, you
cannot touch me for coining', he called me
over. My knees were jelly. "Were you on the
timpani tonight?" "Yes, sir," I said, fearing
the worst. "Thank you," he said. "You're
an artist." I didn't sleep a wink. Next day he
asked if I'd be his dresser.
[*Pause.*]

HER LADYSHIP: My father was exactly the same. Always
exaggerated his illnesses. That's why I
thought it was not very serious, I thought—

NORMAN: Madge. You can always tell. She walks as if
the band were playing Onward Christian
Soldiers.
[MADGE *knocks on dressing room door and
goes in.*]

MADGE: Any further developments?
[HER LADYSHIP *shakes her head.*]
We had better see the manager. Perhaps
you ought to come with me.

NORMAN: Oh, your ladyship, please, let's take our
time, let's not rush things—

MADGE: [*to* HER LADYSHIP] There's no alternative.

HER LADYSHIP: Madge is right, he's in hospital. We can't
play *King Lear* without the King. No one
will pay to see the crucifixion of the two
thieves. We have to make a decision.

NORMAN: Forgive me, your ladyship, it's not a decision
you have to make, it's the right decision.
I had a friend, before one's face was lined,
as the saying goes, in a very low state he was,

ever so fragile, a pain to be with. You weren't safe from him on top of a bus. If he happened to sit beside you, he'd tell you the ABC of unhappiness between request stops. Someone close to him, his mother, I believe, though it was never proved, understandably upset, made a decision. A little rest, she said, among those similarly off-centre, in Colwyn Bay, never a good date, not in February, wrapped in a grey rug, gazing at a grey sea. Talk about bleak. Mother-dear made a decision but it was the wrong decision. My friend never acted again.

MADGE: [*to* HER LADYSHIP] We have to face the facts.

NORMAN: I've never done that in my life, your ladyship, and I don't see why I should start now. I just like things to be lovely. No pain, that's my motto.

MADGE: But things aren't lovely, Norman.

NORMAN: They aren't if you face facts. Face the facts, it's facing the company I worry about. Poor lambs. What'll happen to them? And the customers? There was a queue at the box office this afternoon, if four elderly spinsters constitute a queue. Pity to give them their money back, they've likely had enough disappointment in life as it is. It's no good Sir talking about responsibility and service and struggle and survival and then you go and cancel the performance.

MADGE: [*to* HER LADYSHIP] It's a disease.

HER LADYSHIP: What is?

MADGE: Hopefulness. I think we should discuss this in private. I'll be in my room.

[*She goes.* HER LADYSHIP *is about to follow.*]

NORMAN: Yes, well, perhaps it is a disease, but I've caught something much worse from Sir.

HER LADYSHIP: What?

NORMAN: A bad dose of Holy Grail.

> [*He laughs, but the laughter turns to tears.* HER LADYSHIP *goes to him.*]

HER LADYSHIP: Years ago, in my father's company. The unmentionable Scots tragedy. A new Macduff. Couldn't remember the lines. My father should've sacked him at the end of the first rehearsal. But no, my father said, "He'll know it, he'll know it." He never did.

NORMAN: Oh well, that was the Scots tragedy. Everyone knows that's the unluckiest play in the world. That's the one superstition I believe in absolutely. That play would turn a good fairy wicked.

HER LADYSHIP: In the fight scene. The man couldn't remember the fight. He thrust when he shouldn't have and sliced my father's face across. The right cheek seized up in a lopsided grin. The only part left to my father was Caliban.

NORMAN: It's not the same thing—

HER LADYSHIP: I'll be in Madge's room if I'm wanted.

NORMAN: Don't decide yet, your ladyship, let me go to the hospital, let me see how he is, you never know—

HER LADYSHIP: I do know. I realise now I've witnessed a slow running-down. I've heard the hiss of air escaping. We'll call the company together at the half. I'll tell them—

> [NORMAN *is suddenly alert.*]

—that tonight's performance is cancelled, that the engagement is to be ended—

> [*Heavy footsteps. Both look at each other. Footsteps nearer.* SIR *enters in a dishevelled state. Long pause.*]

NORMAN: Good evening, Sir.

SIR: Good evening, Norman. Good evening, Pussy.

HER LADYSHIP: Bonzo, why are you here?

SIR: My name is on the door.

HER LADYSHIP: Did the doctors say you could leave?

SIR: Doctors? Executioners. Do you know what he told me? A short, bald butcher, *Il Duce* in a white coat. "You need rest," he said. Is that all? When a doctor tells you you need rest, you can be certain he hasn't the slightest idea of what's wrong with you. I discharged myself.

[*He weeps.*]

HER LADYSHIP: [*to* NORMAN] Telephone the hospital.

SIR: Do not telephone the hospital.

[*He continues to weep.*]

HER LADYSHIP: Norman, will you leave us, please?

NORMAN: I'll see Madge and tell her there's an alternative.

[NORMAN *goes. Silence.*]

HER LADYSHIP: [*with real disgust*] You're fit for nothing.

SIR: Please, Pussy, don't.

HER LADYSHIP: Cancel the performance.

SIR: Can't. Mustn't. Won't.

HER LADYSHIP: Then take the consequences.

SIR: When have I not?

HER LADYSHIP: The doctor promised you'd be kept there.

SIR: They tried to inject me. They couldn't hold me down.

HER LADYSHIP: Where have you been all day? Don't tell me you found a brothel in this town.

SIR: I can't remember all I've done. I know towards evening I was being pursued but I couldn't see who the villains were. Then the warning went. I refused to take shelter. I'm accustomed to the blasted heath. Acrid smell. Eyes watering. Wherever I went I seemed to hear a woman crying. Suddenly, I had a clear image of my father on the beach near Lowestoft, plans in his hands, inspecting the boats his men had built. "An actor?" he said, "Never. You will be a boat builder like me." But I defied him and lost his love. Father preferred people to cower. But I had to chart my own course. I decide when I'm ready for the scrap-yard. Not you. I and no one else. I.

    [*He sits and stares.*]

HER LADYSHIP: The woman you heard crying was me.

SIR: [*calling*] Norman! Norman! Norman!

    [NORMAN *comes running down the corridor and goes into the dressing room, followed shortly by* MADGE.]

NORMAN: Sir.

SIR: Norman, I want you by me.

NORMAN: Yes, Sir.

SIR: Don't leave my side, Norman.

NORMAN: No, Sir.

SIR: I shall want help, Norman.

NORMAN: Yes, Sir.

    [MADGE *knocks and enters.*]

SIR: Madge-dear.

HER LADYSHIP: [*to* MADGE] You speak to him. He doesn't hear a word I say. He's obviously incapable—

MADGE: [*to* SIR] You look exhausted.

NORMAN: That's what I call tact.

MADGE: Are you sure you're able to go on tonight?

NORMAN: He wouldn't be here if he wasn't, would you, Sir?

SIR: [*to* MADGE] How long have you been with me, Madge-dear?

MADGE: Longer than anyone else.

SIR: How long?

MADGE: Twenty years, nearly twenty years.

SIR: Have I ever missed a performance?

MADGE: No, but then you've never been ill.

    [SIR *sits and stares.*]

[*quietly*] I only want what's best for you.

NORMAN: What's best for Sir is that he's allowed to get ready.

SIR: Ready, yes, I must get ready.

[*He waves them away.*]

MADGE: Ready for what?

[*She goes.* SIR *sits and stares.*]

NORMAN: Excuse me, your ladyship, shouldn't you be getting ready, too?

[*He puts a kettle on a small gas ring.*]

HER LADYSHIP: I can't bear to see him like that.

NORMAN: Then best to leave us. I've had experience of these things. I know what has to be done.

[SIR *stifles a sob.*]

HER LADYSHIP: Imagine waking to that night after night.

[*She goes.* NORMAN *secretly takes a quarter bottle of brandy from his pocket and has a swig. He replaces the bottle and turns to* SIR.]

NORMAN: Right! Shall we begin at the beginning? [*Pause.*] Good evening, Sir. [*Pause.*] Good evening, Norman. And how are you this evening, Sir? A little tearful, I'm afraid, and you, Norman? I'm very well, thank you, Sir, had ever such a quiet day, cleaning your wig and beard, ironing your costumes, washing your undies. And what have you been up to, Sir? I've been jumping on my hat, Norman. Have you? That's an odd thing to do. May one ask why? Why what, Norman? Why we've been jumping on our hat, Sir? Not much fun for me this conversation, not much fun for you either, I suspect. [*Pause.*] Are we going to sulk all evening, or are we going to speak to our servants? [*Pause.*] I do wish you'd stop crying, Sir. [*Pause.*] Shall we play 'I Spy'? I spy with my little eye something beginning with A. I know you won't guess so I'll tell. A is for actor. And actors have to work, and actors have to put on their make-

up and change their frocks and then, of
course, actors have to act. Zounds, madam,
where dost thou get this knowledge? From a
baboon, Sir, that wandered wild in Eden.
Or words to that effect. I've never known a
kettle take so long to boil. Tell you what,
have a little brandy. Break the rules, have a
nip. A little brandy won't harm as the
surgeon said to the undertaker's widow.

[*No response.* NORMAN *has a nip of brandy
himself.*]

There's less than an hour to go. You usually
want longer. Shall we make a start?

[SIR *looks up at him.*]

Yes, it's me, Norman, the one with the
soulful eyes.

[*The kettle boils.* NORMAN *makes tea.*]

I saved my rations for you. I don't mind
going without.

[*He hums to himself and then takes a cup
to* SIR.]

Drink up. It's tea, not rat poison.

[NORMAN *sits beside* SIR *and feeds him the tea.*
SIR *drinks tea.*]

There. That's better, isn't it? Isn't it?

[SIR *moistens his lips.*]

Would you like a bicky? I saved one from the
mayor's reception in Bridlington. No? Then
why don't you have one, Norman? Thanks
very much, I will.

[*He takes a biscuit from the tin and eats it.*]

If you don't mind my saying so, Sir, there
seems little point in discharging yourself
from hospital, and coming to sit here like
Niobe prior to being turned into stone. So.
Shall we make an effort?

[SIR *tries to loosen his collar and tie.*]

Let me. That's what I'm here for.

[*He helps* SIR, *who suddenly grabs hold of* NORMAN, *buries his face in his neck and sobs.*]
I know how it feels. I had a friend, worse than you he was, and all they ever wanted to do with him was put him away. And no one wants to go through that. Or so my friend said. They'll send you to Colwyn Bay and you know you never do any business in Colwyn Bay. And guess what got my friend well? Sounds silly this. An offer of work. A telegram, yes, fancy, a telegram. Can you understudy Scrubby *Outward Bound* start Monday? He discharged himself, just like you, my friend did, took the train up to London, found digs in Brixton and never looked back. What do you make of that? An offer of work. Meant someone had thought of him and that's ever such a comfort.

[SIR *disengages himself.*]
So here's something to cheer you up. It's going to be a Full House tonight. All those people thinking of you and wanting you to act.

[*Long pause.*]

SIR: Really? A Full House?

NORMAN: Shall we make a start?

[*Long pause.*]

SIR: What play is it tonight?

NORMAN: *King Lear*, Sir.

SIR: Impossible.

NORMAN: Thank you very much, that's nice, isn't it? People paying good money to see you and you say impossible, very nice indeed, I don't think.

[*Pause.*]

SIR: I don't want to be seen.

NORMAN: Difficult when you're playing King Lear with the lighting you use.

SIR: I don't want to see Her Ladyship.

NORMAN: Even more difficult since she's playing Cordelia. You saw her a moment ago. You were alone together.

SIR: Were we? What's the play tonight?

NORMAN: *King Lear,* Sir.

[*Pause.*]

SIR: Madge was wrong.

NORMAN: She often is.

SIR: I have been ill before. Did you ever see me in *The Corsican Brothers*?

NORMAN: Alas no, Sir, before my time.

SIR: I went on with double pneumonia. Apt when you're playing the Corsican Brothers. I'd rather have double pneumonia than this.

NORMAN: Than what?

[SIR *allows* NORMAN *to help him undress.*]

SIR: What prevents me from packing up and going home? Why am I here when I should be asleep? Even kings abdicate.

NORMAN: Well I hope he's happy with the woman he loves, that's all I can say, I hope he's happy. Shall we undress? Talk of undressing, wasn't it a strange light in Market Square this evening?

SIR: I don't remember being in Market Square.

NORMAN: You've been missing the whole day. What do you remember?

SIR: Walking, walking, walking. If only I could find a good, catchy title. I think *My Life* a little plain, don't you?

NORMAN: Still stuck, are we?

SIR: No. I wrote a little today. Two or three sides of an exercise book. But I can't find a title.

NORMAN: We'll think of something.

SIR: See if it's still in my coat. And my reading glasses.

[NORMAN *looks in the pocket of the overcoat,*

                         finds the exercise book and a pair of broken spectacles. He takes the book to SIR *and holds up the spectacles.*]

NORMAN: You won't see much through these.

                         [SIR *pages through the book.*]

SIR: I thought I'd written today. Look for me. Is there anything?

                         [NORMAN *flicks through the pages.*]

No. Evidently not. It can't be *Lear* again?

NORMAN: Shall we begin our make-up?

                         [*He guides* SIR *to the dressing table but* SIR *stops suddenly.*]

SIR: Where's my hat? I'm getting out of here. I'm not staying in this place a moment longer. I'm surrounded by vipers, betrayal on every side. I am being crushed, the life blood is draining out of me. The load is too great. Norman, Norman, if you have any regard for me, don't listen to him—

NORMAN: Who? Who?

SIR: More, more, more, I can't give any more, I have nothing more to give. I want a tranquil senility. I'm a grown man. I don't want to go on painting my face night after night, wearing clothes that are not my own, I'm not a child dressing up for charades, this is my work, my life's work, I'm an actor, and who cares if I go out there tonight or any other night and shorten my life?

                         [*He sits, buries his face in his hands.*]

NORMAN: I had a friend once said, "Norman, I don't care if there are only three people out front, or if the audience laugh when they shouldn't, or don't when they should, one person, just one person is certain to know and under-stand. And I act for him." That's what my friend said.

SIR: I can't move that which can't be moved.

NORMAN: What are we on about now?

SIR: I'm filled inside with stone. Stone upon stone. I can't lift myself. The weight is too much. I know futility when I see it. I dream at night of unseen hands driving wooden stakes into my feet. I can't move, and when I look at the wounds I see a jellied, leprous pus. And the dream is long and graceless. I wake up, sweat-drenched, poisoned. And the whole day long there is a burning heat inside me, driving all else from my mind. What did I do today?

NORMAN: You walked. You thought you wrote. You were in Market Square. A woman kissed your hand and said you were lovely in *The Corsican Brothers.*

SIR: How do you know all this? Has someone been talking?

[*Pause.*]

NORMAN: I don't wish to hurry you, Sir, no, I lie, I do.

SIR: I hate the swines.

NORMAN: Who?

SIR: He's a hard task-master, he drives me too hard. I have too much to carry.

[MADGE *knocks on the door.* NORMAN *opens it but doesn't admit her.*]

NORMAN: Yes?

MADGE: I'd like to see him.

NORMAN: I'd rather you didn't.

MADGE: It's my responsibiity to take the curtain up tonight. There isn't much time.

NORMAN: Things have reached a delicate stage. I don't want him disturbed.

SIR: What's all the whispering?

NORMAN: Nothing, nothing.

MADGE: Has he begun to make up yet?

NORMAN: Not yet but—

MADGE: Do you realise how late it is? They'll be calling the half in a moment.

NORMAN: I know how late it is.

MADGE: Then on your head be it.

[*She goes.*]

SIR: Who was that?

NORMAN: Only Madge to say everything's running like clockwork.

[*He looks anxiously at his watch.*]

Oh, look! A dressing-gown! Shall we put it on and keep ourselves warm?

[*He helps* SIR *on with his dressing-gown.*]

What's it matter where you were or what you did today? You're here, in the theatre, safe and sound, where you belong. And a Full House. Lovely.

SIR: Really? A Full House?

NORMAN: They'll be standing in the gods.

[NORMAN *guides* SIR *to the dressing table.* SIR *sits and stares at himself in the looking-glass.*]

SIR: Do you know they bombed the Grand Theatre, Plymouth?

NORMAN: And much else of the city besides.

SIR: I made my debut at the Grand Theatre, Plymouth.

NORMAN: They weren't to know.

SIR: I shouldn't have come out this autumn, but I had no choice. He made me.

NORMAN: Who?

SIR: I should have rested.

NORMAN: I had a friend who was ordered to rest. He obeyed. That was the end of him. He was ever so ill. Nearly became a Catholic. [*Pause.*] Would you like a little rub-down?

[*No response.*]

I'm not surprised you're feeling dispirited.

It's been ever such a hard time. No young
men to play the juveniles and the trouble
with Mr Davenport-Scott.

[SIR *is suddenly alert.*]

SIR: What news of Mr Davenport-Scott?

NORMAN: The police have opposed bail.

SIR: What?

NORMAN: Well, he'd had his second warning.

SIR: How then do we dispose our forces?

NORMAN: Mr Thornton is standing by to play Fool.

SIR: And who as Oswald?

NORMAN: Mr Browne, I'm afraid.

SIR: That leaves me a Knight short for 'Reason
not the need'.

NORMAN: Ninety-eight short, actually, if you take the
text as gospel, so one more or less won't be
too upsetting.

SIR: Thornton toothless as Fool. Browne lisping
as Oswald. Oxenby limping as Edmund.
What have I come to? I've never had a
company like this one. I'm reduced to old
men, cripples and nancy-boys. Herr Hitler
has made it very difficult for Shakespearean
companies.

NORMAN: It'll be a chapter in the book, Sir. I hate to
mention this but we're going to be short for
the storm. We've no one to operate the wind
machine, not if Mr Thornton is to play Fool.
Mr Thornton was ever so good on the wind
machine. Madge knows the problem but
she's very unsympathetic.

SIR: You tell Madge from me I must have the
storm at full strength. What about Oxenby?

NORMAN: Not the most amenable of gentlemen.

SIR: Send him to me at the half. I'll have a word
with him. And I'd better talk to Thornton,
too.

NORMAN: You see? That's more like it. You're where

you belong, doing what you know best, and you're yourself again. You start making up. I'll go and tell them to come and see you. I've cleaned the wig and beard. I'll see what we can do with these. Jumping on his hat indeed! Shan't be a minute.

[NORMAN *goes.* SIR *looks at himself, then begins to black up.* NORMAN *returns.*]

Oh no, Sir! No! Not Othello!

[SIR *looks at him helplessly;* NORMAN *begins to clean his face with cold cream.*]

SIR: The lines are fouled. Up on your short, down on your long. Do we have a dead for it? Instruct the puppeteer to renew the strings. The stuffing's escaping at the seams, straw from a scarecrow lies scattered down stage left.

[NORMAN *cleans* SIR*'s face.*]

NORMAN: I'd have given anything to see the play tonight. There's you all blacked up and Cordelia saying, "You begot me, bred me, loved me." Well, you see, ducky, this King Lear has been about a bit.

[SIR *laughs.*]

SIR: We used to have a game when I was with Benson. We called it *Risqué.* You had to turn the line to get a *double entendre.* The best I ever heard was from a character man called Berriton. You know the line, "What fifty of my followers at a clap? Within a fortnight!"

NORMAN: Yes, I know the line, and the story.

SIR: One day, on the train call between Aberdeen and Liverpool, a journey I recommend as punishment for deserters, Berriton came out with, "What, fifty of my followers with the clap? Within a fortnight!"

[*They both laugh.* NORMAN *has wiped* SIR*'s*

                  face clean. SIR *falls silent. He looks at himself
in the looking-glass.*]

                Another blank page.

NORMAN: The time has come, if you don't mind my saying so, to stop waxing poetical and to wax a bit more practical.

               [*Pause.* SIR *reaches out for a stick of make-up. Knock on the door.*]

NORMAN: Who?

IRENE: Irene. I've come for the triple crown.

SIR: Enter.

               [IRENE, *dressed as a map-bearer in* Lear, *enters.*]

               [*smiles*] Good evening, my child.

IRENE: Good evening, Sir.

SIR: All well?

IRENE: Thank you, Sir.

SIR: You've come for the triple crown.

IRENE: Yes, Sir.

SIR: Polish it well. I like it gleaming.

IRENE: Yes, Sir.

SIR: And return it to me well before curtain up. I like it on my head by the quarter.

IRENE: Yes, Sir.

SIR: And when I've used it on stage, see that it's returned to my room after the interval.

NORMAN: She has done it before, Sir.

SIR: I like to be certain. Here it is, my child.

               [*She comes to him. He pats her bottom.*]

               Pretty young thing, aren't you?

IRENE: Thank you, Sir.

               [*She goes.* SIR *stares fondly into space.*]

NORMAN: Sir, it's time to age.

               [SIR *looks at his make-up tray.*]

SIR: [*in a panic*] They're all the same colour. Which stick do I use? I can't see the colours.

               [*He looks at* NORMAN *helplessly.* NORMAN

> *goes to the basin and ewer, pours water, wets*
> *a bar of soap, and brings it to* SIR.]

NORMAN: You start with the eyebrows.

SIR: Eyebrows?

NORMAN: Yes, Sir. You soap the eyebrows.

> [SIR *applies soap to his eyebrows so that they*
> *are flattened.*]

Good. Now Number Five.

> [*He hands* SIR *the stick.*]

Just the mask you always say. Leave clean
the upper lip and chin for the moustache and
beard. And not too high on the forehead.

> [SIR *applies the greasepaint.*]

There. Easy as falling off a tightrope.

> [SIR *continues to make up.*]

SIR: In a Pythagorean future life I should certainly
take up painting. My palette, a few brushes,
a three-and-sixpenny canvas, a camp stool
and no one to drive you.

NORMAN: No one drives you but yourself.

SIR: How dare you, how would you know, who
says I drive myself? I'm driven, driven,
driven—

NORMAN: I'm sorry, I didn't mean—

SIR: You have to believe in yourself and your
destiny, you have to keep faith with your
aspirations and allow yourself to be enslaved
by them, and the bondage is everlasting.
How dare you!

NORMAN: I'm sorry I mentioned it—

SIR: You have to learn to wait and wait and wait,
and the moment comes when you launch
your barque and take the rudder, then, oh
my masters! beware. The effort to forget all
you are risking, to face a first night audience
before whom to lay open your soul, to put
your entire life in jeopardy time after time,
to bear your back to the stripes of the critics,

to go on doing these things year after year,
always with the terror increasing, because it's
easier to climb than it is to hang on, and now
d'you see why Benson wrote me after my first
essay into management, "May you have the
health and strength to go on"? On and on
and on.

NORMAN: You should put that in the book.

SIR: Do they know what it means? Do they care?
I hate the swines.

NORMAN: Who?

SIR: On and on and on—

NORMAN: All right, Sir, shall we go on and on and on
with our make-up?

> [*Pause.* SIR *looks helplessly at his make-up
> tray.*]

Lake for the lines.

> [NORMAN *hands* SIR *a stick of lake.* SIR *begins
> to apply the lines.*]

SIR: There was a time when I had to paint in all
the lines. Now I merely deepen what is
already there.

> [*He continues to make up.* MADGE *comes to
> the door, and knocks.* NORMAN *answers it.*]

NORMAN: What now?

MADGE: How is he?

NORMAN: He'll be all right if he's left in peace.

MADGE: I want to see with my own eyes.

NORMAN: He is not to be disturbed.

MADGE: And what about the understudies?

NORMAN: He knows all about it, everything's in hand.

MADGE: The manager wants to know if he can let the
house in.

NORMAN: Tell him yes.

MADGE: You realise now there's going to be an
audience out there.

NORMAN: It'd be silly going through all this if there
wasn't.

MADGE: Will he be ready on time? Will he be well
           enough?

NORMAN: Yes.

           [*He closes the door on her.*]

SIR: What is going on, who was that?

NORMAN: Just a minion, minioning.

SIR: Too many interruptions—my concentra-
           tion—Norman!

NORMAN: Sir?

SIR: How does the play begin?

NORMAN: Which play, Sir?

SIR: Tonight's, tonight's, I can't remember my
           first line.

NORMAN: 'Attend the Lords of France and Burgundy,
           Gloucester.'

SIR: Yes, yes. What performance is this?

           [NORMAN *consults a small notebook.*]

NORMAN: Tonight will be your two hundred and
           twenty-seventh performance of the part, Sir.

SIR: Two hundred and twenty-seven Lears and I
           can't remember the first line.

NORMAN: We've forgotten something, if you don't
           mind my saying so.

           [SIR *looks at him blankly.*]
           We have to sink our cheeks.

           [SIR *applies the appropriate make-up.*]

SIR: I shall look like this in my coffin.

NORMAN: And a broad straight line of Number Twenty
           down the nose. Gives strength, you say.

           [SIR *adds the line down the nose and studies the*
           result. NORMAN *pours a little Brown and*
           Polson's cornflour into a bowl.]

SIR: Were you able to find any Brown and
           Polson's?

NORMAN: No, but I'm still looking. There's enough left
           for this tour. Now, we mix the white hard
           varnish with a little surgical spirit, don't we?

SIR: I know how to stick on a beard. I have been a

depictor for over forty years and steered my
own course for over thirty. You think I don't
know how to affix a beard and moustache?
You overstep the mark, boy. Don't get above
yourself.

> [SIR *begins to apply the gum, and stick on the
> beard.* NORMAN *turns his back and has a nip
> of brandy.*]

I shall want a rest after the storm scene.

NORMAN: There's no need to tell me. I know.

SIR: Towel.

> [NORMAN *hands* SIR *a towel which* SIR *presses
> against the beard and moustache.* SIR *looks at
> himself in the looking-glass, and suddenly
> goes blank.*]

Something's missing. What's missing?

NORMAN: I don't want to get above myself, Sir, but
how about the wig?

> [NORMAN *removes the wig from the block and
> hands it to* SIR.]

And shall we take extra care with the join
tonight? On Tuesday Richard III looked as if
he were wearing a peaked cap.

> [SIR *puts on the wig and begins to colour the
> join. He stops—*]

SIR: Hot, unbearably hot, going to faint—

> [NORMAN *whips out the brandy bottle.*]

NORMAN: Have a nip, it won't harm—

> [SIR *waves him away.* NORMAN *has a nip,
> puts the bottle away, and returns to* SIR *who
> hasn't moved.*]

Oh, Sir, we mustn't give up, not now, not
now. Let's highlight our lines.

> [*Silence.* SIR *continues to add highlights.*]

SIR: Imagine bombing the Grand Theatre,
Plymouth. Barbarians. [*Pause.*] I shall give
them a good one tonight. [*Pause.* SIR *becomes
alarmed.*] Norman!

NORMAN: Sir?

SIR: What's the first line again? All this clitter-clatter-chitter-chatter—

NORMAN: 'Attend the Lords of France and Burgundy—'

SIR: You've put it from my head. You must keep silent when I'm dressing. I have work to do, work, hard bloody labour, I have to carry the world tonight, the whole bloody universe—

NORMAN: Sir, Sir—

SIR: I can't remember the first line. A hundred thousand performances behind me and I have to ask you for the first line—

NORMAN: I'll take you through it—

SIR: Take me through it? Nobody takes you through it, you're *put* through it, night after night, and I haven't the strength.

NORMAN: Well, you're a fine one, I must say, you of all people, you disappoint me, if you don't mind my saying so. You, who always say self-pity is the most unattractive quality on stage or off. Who have you been working for all these years? The Ministry of Information? Struggle and survival, you say, that's all that matters, you say, struggle and survival. Well, we all bloody struggle, don't we? I struggle, I struggle, you think it's easy for me, well, I'll tell you something for nothing it isn't easy, not one little bit, neither the struggle nor the bloody survival. The whole world's struggling for bloody survival, so why can't you?

[*Silence.*]

SIR: My dear Norman, I seem to have upset you. I apologise. I understand. We cannot always be strong. There are dangers in covering the cracks.

NORMAN: Never mind about covering the cracks, what about the wig join?

[SIR *continues to make up.*]

I'm sorry if I disturbed your concentration.

SIR: 'We both understand servitude, Alfonso.' What came next? What did I say to that?

NORMAN: 'Was it lack of ambition allowed me to endure what I have had to endure? It depends, your highness, what is meant by ambition. If ambition means a desire to sit in the seats of the mighty, yes, I have lacked such ambition. To me it has been a matter of some indifference where I have done my work. It has been the work itself which has been my chief joy.'

SIR: A fine memory, Norman.

NORMAN: My memory's like a policeman. Never there when you want it.

SIR: That was a play. And a money-maker. Greatly admired by clever charwomen and stupid clergymen. If I was twenty years younger I could still go on acting that kind of rubbish. But now I have to ascend the cosmos. And do they care? I hate the swines.

NORMAN: Shall we finish our eyebrows?

[SIR *combs the soaped eyebrows and whitens them.* IRENE *knocks on the door.*]

IRENE: Half an hour, please, Sir.

[*She goes.*]

SIR: Already?

NORMAN: You were late in tonight, Sir.

SIR: Why hasn't she returned the triple crown? I like it on my head by now. Look!

NORMAN: What?

SIR: My hands. They're shaking.

NORMAN: Very effective in the part. Don't forget to make them up.

SIR: I can't keep them still. Do it for me.

[NORMAN *holds up his own hand, which is trembling.*]

NORMAN: Look, it must be infectious.

       [NORMAN *makes up* SIR*'s hands.*]

SIR: I can face the division of my kingdom. I can cope with Fool. I can bear the reduction of my retinue. I can stomach the curses I have to utter. I can even face being whipped by the storm. But I dread the final entrance. To carry on Cordelia dead, to cry like the wind, howl, howl, howl. To lay her gently on the ground. To die. Have I the strength?

NORMAN: If you haven't the strength, no one has.

SIR: You're a good friend, Norman.

NORMAN: Thank you, Sir.

SIR: What would I do without you?

NORMAN: Manage on your own, I expect.

SIR: You'll be rewarded.

NORMAN: Pardon me while I get my violin.

SIR: Don't mock me. I may not have long.

NORMAN: My father used to say that. Lived to be ninety-three. May still be alive for all I know. There! Albert Dürer couldn't have done better.

       [*He rises. He powders* SIR*'s hands.* HER LADYSHIP *enters, wigged and costumed as Cordelia but wearing a dressing-gown.*]

HER LADYSHIP: Bonzo, how do you feel?

SIR: A little more myself, Pussy.

NORMAN: You see? Once he's assumed the disguise, he's a different man. Egad, Madam, thou hast a porcupine wit.

HER LADYSHIP: And you're sure you're able to go on?

SIR: On and on and on.

NORMAN: Don't start that again, please.

SIR: Pussy, I thought it was the Black One tonight.

HER LADYSHIP: My dear.

SIR: Pussy, did I wake in the night? Did I thank you for watching over me? Was there talk of violence?

[*Pause.*]

HER LADYSHIP: No, Bonzo, you dreamt it.

SIR: I still have the feeling.

HER LADYSHIP: Shall I fetch the cloak and tie it on as usual?

SIR: Yes. As usual.

HER LADYSHIP: Mr Thornton and Mr Oxenby are waiting outside to see you. Shall I ask them to come in?

SIR: I don't want to see Oxenby. He frightens me. Mind you, he's the best Iago I've ever had or seen and I include that four-foot-six ponce Sir Arthur Palgrove.

NORMAN: [*to* HER LADYSHIP] That's more like the Sir we know and love.

SIR: *Sir* Arthur Palgrove. He went on playing Hamlet till he was sixty-eight. There were more lines on his face than steps to the gallery. I saw his Lear. I was pleasantly disappointed. *Sir* Arthur Palgrove. Who advises His Majesty, answer me that?

[*He continues to adjust his make-up, putting the finishing touches.* HER LADYSHIP *draws* NORMAN *aside.*]

HER LADYSHIP: You're a miracle-worker, Norman.

NORMAN: Thank you, your ladyship.

HER LADYSHIP: Here's a piece of chocolate for you.

NORMAN: Thank you, your ladyship.

HER LADYSHIP: It'll be all hands to the pump tonight, Norman.

NORMAN: A small part of the service, your ladyship.

HER LADYSHIP: Thank you.

[*She goes.*]

SIR: Don't suppose I didn't see that because I did. There are thousands of children in this beloved land of ours scavenging the larders for something sweet, and if only they came to me I could tell them of the one person in England who has an inexhaustible supply of

chocolate. It is *I* who have to carry her on
dead as Cordelia. It is *I* who have to lift her
up, carry her in my arms. Thank Christ,
I thought, for rationing, but no, she'd find
sugar in a sand-dune.

NORMAN: Shall I show the actors in?

SIR: I don't—I don't want—

NORMAN: Sir, you have to see the actors.

> [*He opens the door and calls:*]

Mr Thornton!

> [GEOFFREY THORNTON, *an elderly actor,
> enters. He wears a costume as Fool that is
> much too large for him.*]

Mr Thornton to see you, Sir.

SIR: Well, Geoffrey...does the costume fit?

GEOFFREY: Mr Davenport-Scott was such a tall man.

SIR: Mr Davenport-Scott was a worm. You look—

> [*He makes a vague gesture.* NORMAN *begins to
> help* SIR *into his Lear costume.*]

Do you know the lines?

GEOFFREY: Yes.

SIR: Don't keep me waiting for them.

GEOFFREY: Oh no.

SIR: Pace, pace, pace, pace, pace, pace.

GEOFFREY: Yes.

SIR: And keep out of my focus.

GEOFFREY: Yes.

SIR: The boom lights placed in the downstage
wings are for me and me only.

GEOFFREY: Yes, old man, I know.

SIR: You must find what light you can.

GEOFFREY: Right.

SIR: Let me hear you sing.

GEOFFREY: What?

SIR: 'He that has and a little tiny wit.'

GEOFFREY: [*faltering*] 'He that has and—he that has—'

NORMAN: [*singing*] 'He that has and a little tiny wit...'

GEOFFREY: 'He that has and a little tiny wit,

> With hey, ho, the wind and the rain,
> Must make content with his fortunes fit,
> For the rain it raineth every day.'

SIR: All right, speak it, don't sing it. And in the storm scene, if you're going to put your arms round my legs as Davenport-Scott did, then round my calves not my thighs. He nearly ruptured me twice.

GEOFFREY: If you rather I didn't, old man—

SIR: Feel it, my boy, feel it, that's the only way. Whatever takes you.

GEOFFREY: Right.

SIR: But do not let too much take you. Remain within the bounds. And at all costs remain still when I speak.

GEOFFREY: Of course.

SIR: And no crying in the part.

GEOFFREY: Oh no.

SIR: *I* have the tears in this play.

GEOFFREY: I know.

SIR: Serve the playwright.

GEOFFREY: Yes.

SIR: And keep your teeth in.

GEOFFREY: It's only when I'm nervous—

SIR: You will be nervous, I guarantee it. There will be no extra payment for this performance. I believe your contract is 'play as cast'.

GEOFFREY: Yes.

SIR: Good fortune attend your endeavours.

GEOFFREY: Thank you, Sir.

> [SIR *nods for him to leave.* NORMAN *sees him out.*]

NORMAN: God bless, Geoffrey.

GEOFFREY: I'd rather face the Nazi hordes any time.

> [*He goes.*]

SIR: I hope Mr Churchill has better men in the Cabinet.

NORMAN: Mr Oxenby's waiting, Sir.

SIR: Oxenby? What—what—I can't—what does Oxenby want?

NORMAN: It's not what he wants, it's what we want, someone to operate the wind machine—

SIR: I don't want to see Oxenby, I can't bear the man, it's stifling in here—

NORMAN: We'll have no storm without him.

[*Silence.* NORMAN *admits* OXENBY, *dressed as Edmund. He limps. Pause.*]

Mr Oxenby to see you, Sir.

OXENBY: You wanted to see me.

SIR: I—I did I? I—Norman—why—?

NORMAN: Sir was wondering whether he could ask of you a favour.

OXENBY: He can ask.

NORMAN: You haven't been with us very long but I'm sure you've seen enough to know that we're not so much a company as one big happy family. We all muck in as required. As you will no doubt have heard, Mr Davenport-Scott will not be rejoining the company.

OXENBY: Yes, I've heard. You share a dressing-room with one or two of them, you hear nothing else. It upsets the pansy fraternity when one of their number is caught.

NORMAN: Because Mr Thornton is having to play Fool, and because our two elderly Knights are setting the hovel behind the front cloth during the storm, we have no one to operate the wind machine. We'd ask Mr Browne but he's really rather too fragile. We wondered if you would turn the handle.

OXENBY: In short, no.

[*Silence.*]

Anything else?

[*No response.*]

Has he read my play yet?

[*No response.* OXENBY *goes.*]

SIR: Perhaps the Russians have had a setback on the Eastern front. Bolshevism will be the ruin of the theatre.

NORMAN: What are we going to do? Fancy not wanting to muck in.

SIR: He hates me. I feel his hatred. All I stand for he despises. I wouldn't read his play, not if he were Commissar of Culture.

NORMAN: I've read it.

SIR: Is there a part for me?

NORMAN: Yes, but you wouldn't credit the language. The Lord Chamberlain would get lockjaw.

SIR: He was ungenerous about Davenport-Scott. I hold no brief for buggers but where's the man's humanity? A fellow artist brought low and in the cells cannot be cause for rejoicing. I can see exactly what Oxenby's up to. He's writing plays for critics, not people.

NORMAN: Oughtn't we to be quiet for a bit, Sir?

SIR: Where's the girl with the triple crown?

NORMAN: Don't fuss. I'll go and find her.

[NORMAN *goes. Immediately,* IRENE *slips in with the polished triple crown.*]

SIR: Ah, my dear. Norman's just gone to find you.

IRENE: Has he? I must have missed him.

[*She goes close to him, holds out the crown and smiles.*]

SIR: Remind me of your name, my child.

IRENE: Irene, Sir.

SIR: Irene. Charming. Were you at the R.A.D.A.?

IRENE: No, Sir. I went straight into rep.

SIR: Of course. I remember. [*Pause.*] Which rep?

IRENE: Maidenhead.

SIR: Maidenhead. Yes.

[*He takes the crown, puts it down and takes her face in his hands.*]

SIR: Next week. In Eastbourne—

[NORMAN *returns.*]

NORMAN: I can't find her—
  [*He stops.*]
SIR: Just admiring her bone structure.
NORMAN: Run along, Irene.
SIR: Yes, run along.
  [*She goes.*]
  A born actress. Always tell by the cheek bones.
NORMAN: Put on the crown. It's nearly the quarter. Shall I fetch Her Ladyship and ask her to tie on the cloak?
SIR: How does the play begin, God help me, that child has driven it from my mind—
  [MADGE *knocks and enters.*]
MADGE: Quarter of an hour, please, a few minutes late, I'm sorry, that girl, Irene—
SIR: The quarter, I can't, I'm not ready, tell them to go home, give them their money back, I can't, I hate the swines, I can't—I can't—
MADGE: What are you saying, do you want the performance cancelled?
NORMAN: No he doesn't—
SIR: How does it begin?
MADGE: For your own good—
SIR: How does it begin—?
MADGE: You'll never get through it—
NORMAN: He will, he will—
SIR: How does it begin?
NORMAN: Get out, he'll be good and ready when the curtain goes up—
MADGE: We've run out of time.
NORMAN: There's twenty minutes yet. We'll go up late, if necessary.
SIR: Leave me in peace! I can't remember the lines.
  [MADGE *goes.*]
  Norman, Norman, how does it begin?

NORMAN: 'He hath been out nine years and away he shall again.'

> [*Imitates trumpet fanfare.*]

'The King is coming.'

> [*Silence.*]

'Attend the Lords of France and Burgundy, Gloucester.'

SIR: 'Attend the Lords of France and Burgundy, Gloucester.'

NORMAN: 'I shall, my liege.'

> [*Pause.*]

SIR: Yes?

NORMAN: 'Meantime we shall express our darker—'

SIR: 'Meantime we shall express our darker purpose.'

> [*Pause.*]

NORMAN: 'Give me the map—'

SIR: Don't tell me, don't tell me, I know it, I'll ask for it if I need it, I have played the part before, you know. 'Meantime we shall express our darker purpose.'

> [*Long pause.*]

Yes?

NORMAN: 'Give me the map there.'

SIR: 'Give me the map there.' Don't tell me, don't tell me.

> [*Long silence.*]

'What do I fear?'

NORMAN: Wrong. 'Know that we have divided—'

SIR: [*continuing*] 'Myself? there's none else by. True, I talk of dreams, which are the children of an idle brain.'

NORMAN: Wrong play, wrong play—

SIR: 'I will move storms, I will condole in some measure—'

NORMAN: That's another wrong play—

SIR: 'I pray you all, tell me what they deserve

that do conspire my death with devilish plots
of damned witchcraft, and that have prevail'd
upon my body with their hellish charms? Can
this cockpit hold the vasty fields of France?
Men should be what they seem. Macbeth
shall sleep no more! I have lived long
enough!'

NORMAN: Now look what you've gone and done—

SIR: What—?

NORMAN: Go out, go out, you've quoted the Scots
tragedy—

SIR: Did I? Macb—? Did I? Oh Christ—

NORMAN: Out—

> [SIR *goes.*]

Turn round three times. Knock.

> [SIR *turns and knocks.*]

Come in.

> [SIR *re-enters.*]

Swear.

SIR: Pisspots.

> [SIR *holds his head and stands swaying
> slightly.* NORMAN *looks at him despairingly.*
> HER LADYSHIP *enters carrying a cloak and
> dressed as Cordelia.* SIR *looks at her and takes
> her face in his hands.*]

'And my poor fool is hang'd. No, no, no life!
Why should a dog, a horse, a rat have life
And thou no breath at all?
Thou'lt come no more.
Never, never, never, never, never!'

> [*Silence.*]

NORMAN: Welcome back, Sir, you'll be all right.

> [SIR *puts on the triple crown.* HER LADYSHIP
> *puts the cloak around* SIR's *shoulders. A ritual:*]

HER LADYSHIP: [*kissing his hand*] Struggle, Bonzo.

SIR: [*kissing her hand*] Survival, Pussy.

> [*Knock on door.*]

IRENE: [*off*] Five minutes, please, Sir.

NORMAN: Thank you

SIR: Let us descend and survey the scene of battle.

[*They are about to go when the air-raid sirens sound. They freeze.*]

The night I played my first Lear there was a real thunderstorm. Now they send bombs. How much more have I to endure? We are to speak Will Shakespeare tonight and they will go to any lengths to prevent me.

NORMAN: I shouldn't take it so personally, Sir—

SIR: [*looking heavenward*] Bomb, bomb, bomb us into oblivion if you dare, but each word I speak will be a shield against your savagery, each line I utter protection from your terror.

NORMAN: I don't think they can hear you, Sir.

SIR: Swines! Barbarians!

[SIR *begins to shiver uncontrollably, and to whimper.*]

NORMAN: Oh Sir, just as we were winning.

HER LADYSHIP: Perhaps it's timely. He can't go on. Look at him.

[*She comforts him.*]

[*to* NORMAN] Fetch Madge.

SIR: Norman!

NORMAN: Sir.

SIR: Get me down to the stage. By Christ, no squadron of Fascist-Bolsheviks will stop me now.

[*He continues to shiver.* HER LADYSHIP *and* NORMAN *look at each other uncertainly.*]

Do as I say!

[NORMAN *and* HER LADYSHIP *help him.*]

HER LADYSHIP: Who'll make the announcement?

SIR: Davenport-Scott, of course.

[*Silence.*]

NORMAN: Oh dear. Mr Davenport-Scott isn't here tonight. Everyone else is in costume.

SIR: You then Norman.

NORMAN: Me, Sir? No, Sir. I can't appear!

SIR: You, Norman.

NORMAN: But, Sir, I shall never remember what to say—

SIR: Do not argue, I have given my orders, I have enough to contend with—

NORMAN: But, Sir, Sir, I'm not equipped.

SIR: Do it.

> [HER LADYSHIP *helps him. As they go*—]

Why can't I stop shaking?

> [*Sirens continue loudly. Bombs begin to fall.* NORMAN *swigs deeply from the brandy bottle and finishes it. Sirens. Bomb. Blackout. Sirens and bombs continue. A bright spotlight on* NORMAN.]

NORMAN: [*softly*] Ladies and gentlemen…[*louder*] Ladies and gentlemen, the—the warning has just gone. An air-raid is in progress. We shall proceed with the performance. Will those—will those who wish to live—will those who wish to leave do so as quietly as possible? Thank you.

> [*He stands rooted to the spot. Bombs.*]

> [*Blackout.*]

END OF ACT ONE

ACT TWO

The wings. Darkness. The air-raid continues.
NORMAN'*s voice is heard.*

NORMAN: [*softly*] Ladies and gentlemen…[*louder*] Ladies
and gentlemen, the—the warning has just
gone. An air-raid is in progress. We shall
proceed with the performance. Will those—
will those who wish to live—will those who
wish to leave do so as quietly as possible?
Thank you.
> [*Sound of string quartet playing finale of
> selections from 'The Mikado'. Light on*
> MADGE *in prompt corner. Music ends.
> Applause.*]

MADGE: Stand by. Stand by on tabs. House lights
to a half.
> [*She peers through peep-hole at the auditorium.
> Expectant murmurs from audience.*]

Cue timpani.
> [*Timpani starts a steady beat.*]

House lights out.
> [*Pause.*]

Cueing grams.
> [*A recorded fanfare sounds.*]

Cue drum roll.
> [*Timpani breaks into a roll.* MADGE *cues
> tabs.*]

Stand by on stage. Go Elex. Curtain going
up.
> [*Light grows to reveal* NORMAN, *who is carry-
> ing a whip, a towel and a tray on which stands
> a glass of stout and a powder puff. He is just
> entering the wings.*]

[*The following continues onstage at the same time as the play begins offstage.*]

NORMAN: Geoffrey, was I all right? The announcement. Was I effective?

GEOFFREY: Oh yes, old man, damn good.

NORMAN: Your ladyship, was I all right?

HER LADYSHIP: Better than Mr Davenport-Scott.

NORMAN: Really? Do you mean it? I was ever so nervous. Do you think anyone noticed the fluff? "Will those who wish to live." Could have kicked myself. Was I really all right?

HER LADYSHIP: You were fine.

NORMAN: Did he say anything?

HER LADYSHIP: No.

[Offstage we hear the voices of GLOUCESTER, KENT *and* OXENBY *(as Edmund) as they begin the play.]*

KENT

I thought the King had more affected the Duke of Albany . than Cornwall.

GLOUCESTER

It did always seem so to us...

KENT

Is not this your son, my Lord?

GLOUCESTER

His breeding, sir, hath been at my charge: I have so often blushed to acknowledge him, that now I am brazed to it.

KENT

I cannot conceive you.

GLOUCESTER

Sir, this young fellow's mother could; whereupon she grew round-wombed...

GLOUCESTER

But I have a son, sir, by order of law, some year elder than this, who yet is no dearer in my account... Do you know this noble gentleman, Edmund?

EDMUND

No, my Lord.

GLOUCESTER

My Lord of Kent; remember him hereafter as my honourable friend.

MADGE: Cueing grams.
[*Fanfare.*]

MADGE: Stand by please, your ladyship, stand by please, Sir.
[*Fanfare. Trumpet sounds from prompt speaker.* HER LADYSHIP *goes on. Scattered applause.*]

MADGE: Cueing timpani, Sir.
[MADGE *flicks a switch. The green cue light goes on.* IRENE *begins to beat the timpani in a slow rhythm.* MADGE *flicks the switch repeatedly, which makes the green light flash.* IRENE *increases the rhythm of the timpani.*]

MADGE: Stand by, Sir. Cueing the King's fanfare.
[*A great fanfare sounds.* NORMAN *tries to help* SIR *to rise.* SIR *remains seated and continues to shiver.*]

NORMAN: Sir, it's your cue.
[SIR *does not move.* IRENE *continues to drum.*]

NORMAN: Her Ladyship's entered. Quite a nice round, too, Now it's your turn. Come along, Sir.
[*The fanfare ends.* SIR *still does not move.* MADGE *switches off cue light and* IRENE *stops drumming.* MADGE *goes to* SIR *and* NORMAN.]

MADGE: You see? What did I say.

NORMAN: Please, Sir, I implore you.

NORMAN: Sir you're on. You're on.
[*Both* MADGE *and* NORMAN *try to get him on.*]

EDMUND

My services to your lordship.

KENT

I must love you, and sue to know you better.

EDMUND

Sir, I shall study deserving.

GLOUCESTER

He hath been out nine years, and away he shall again...

GLOUCESTER

The King is coming.

GLOUCESTER

The King is coming.
                    [*Silence.*]

OXENBY

Methought I saw the King.

NORMAN: Please, Sir, it's your entrance. Mr Oxenby's having to extemporise.

  [*They try to get* SIR *to his feet. He shivers uncontrollably.*]

NORMAN: Sir, the natives are getting restless. [*to* MADGE] Sound the fanfare again.

  [MADGE *goes to* IRENE *and whispers instructions.* NORMAN *hoists* SIR *to his feet.*]

  [SIR *sits again.*]

  [*A bomb explodes quite close.* NORMAN *gets* SIR *to his feet again and guides him towards the stage.*]

  [OXENBY *comes into the wings from the stage.*]
OXENBY: Is he coming or isn't he?
NORMAN: Yes!

  [OXENBY *goes back on.*]

MADGE: Cue the King's fanfare again.

KENT

Methought so, too.

OXENBY

Methought I saw him, his procession formed, a hundred
knights his escort, sombre they looked, their muted colours
of a tone with the bleak heathland which is our kingdom.

HER LADYSHIP

The King, my father, was, methought, behind me. From
our camp we marched, a goodly distance, I ahead, as is our
custom. Perchance he rested, for age has not the spring
of youth.

[*Murmurs from the audience.*]

OXENBY

Ah! Methinks I see the King.

OXENBY

No, I was mistook.

OXENBY

My Lord, with thy consent I shall to his majestic side, there
to discover his royal progress.

OXENBY

I am assured, my Lord, the King *is* coming.

[*The fanfare sounds. Another bomb explodes quite close.*]

NORMAN: Struggle and survival, Sir, it's a full house.

[SIR *comes to himself.*]

NORMAN: 'Attend the Lords of France and Burgundy, Gloucester.' [*to* MADGE] Cue the Knights, cue the Knights.

MADGE: [*to the* KNIGHTS] Go on. Go on.

[*She switches off the cue light.* IRENE *stops beating, runs to collect the map and stands by for her entrance.*]

NORMAN: [*to* IRENE] Enter, for God's sake.

[IRENE *goes on.* SIR *stands as if poised on a cliff's edge. Then he marches on. Great applause. Silence.* NORMAN *and* MADGE *watch anxiously.*]

[NORMAN *takes out a fresh quarter bottle of brandy and drinks deeply.*]

[*Blackout.*]

[*Bombs and anti-aircraft guns continue. Dim light.* NORMAN, MADGE, GEOFFREY *and others watch the stage and hear* SIR'S *voice.*]

SIR

Attend the Lords of France and Burgundy, Gloucester.

GLOUCESTER

I shall, my liege.

SIR

Meantime we shall express our darker purpose.
Give me the map there...

SIR

No, you unnatural hags,
I will have such revenges on you both
That all the world shall—I will do such things—
What they are yet I know not—but they shall be
The terrors of the earth. You think I'll weep;
No, I'll not weep:

[*The green light glows and* NORMAN *cracks the thunder sheet. The air-raid continues as* SIR *returns to the wings.*]

[*Lights.*]

MADGE: Stand by the storm.

[*The 'All-Clear' sounds.*]
SIR: [*looking heavenwards*] Swines! Just when you need them they run away.

MADGE: Go storm.
[*She switches a switch. The red cue light glows.*]

[*Green warning light. The thunder begins,* NORMAN *and* IRENE *managing between them.* SIR *and* GEOFFREY *go on.*]

[HER LADYSHIP *watches the stage.* OXENBY *stands apart, also watching.* HER LADYSHIP *runs to the thunder crew.*]
HER LADYSHIP: Louder! Louder!
[*She returns to watch the stage as the thunder increases.* HER LADYSHIP *returns to the crew.*]
Louder, louder, he wants it louder!
[*The noise increases.* NORMAN *works*

I have full cause of weeping, but this heart
Shall break into a hundred thousand flaws
Or ere I'll weep. O fool! I shall go mad.

KENT

For confirmation that I am much more
Than my out-wall, open this purse, and take
What it contains. If you shall see Cordelia—
As doubt not but you shall—show her this ring,
And she will tell you who your fellow is
That yet you do not know. Fie on this storm!
I will go seek the King.

GENTLEMAN

Give me your hand. Have you no more to say?

KENT

Few words, but, to effect, more than all yet;
That, when we have found the King—in which your pain
That way, I'll this—he that first lights on him
Holla the other.

SIR

Blow, winds, and crack your cheeks...!
                    [*His voice is drowned by the noise of the
                    storm.*]

frantically. HER LADYSHIP *comes to them again.*]

Louder! Louder!

[NORMAN *and* IRENE *give all they have.* OXENBY, *who has been watching them, takes over the thunder sheet.* HER LADYSHIP *takes charge of the wind machine. The sound of a mighty tempest is reproduced. And when the sound is overpowering and at its loudest: blackout.*]

[SIR *comes raging into the wings. Lights on* SIR *and* NORMAN.]

SIR: [*mad with rage*] *Where was the storm?* I ask for cataracts and hurricanes and I am given trickles and whistles. I demand oak-cleaving thunderbolts and you answer with farting flies. I *am* the storm! I am the wind and the spit and the fire and the pother and I am fed with nothing but muffled funeral drums. Christ Almighty, God forgive them for they know not what they do. I am driven deaf by whispers. Norman, Norman, you have thwarted me.

[SIR *marches into his dressing room followed by* NORMAN.]

I was there, within sight, I had only to be spurred upwards and the glory was mine for the plucking and there was nought, zero, silence, a breeze, a shower, a collision of cotton-wool, the flapping of butterfly wings. I want a tempest not a drizzle. Something will have to be done. I demand to know what happened tonight to the storm!

[SIR *sinks down on to his couch.*]

NORMAN: I'm pleased you're pleased. I've never known you not complain when you've really been at it, and tonight, one could say without fear of contradiction, you were at it. Rest now.

[SIR *lies back.* NORMAN *covers him with a rug, mops his brow and makes him comfortable. Then he turns gas ring up so that kettle boils, makes* SIR *tea and feeds it to him.*]

You've the interval and all Gloucester's blinding before, 'No, they cannot touch me for coining.' Try to sleep. You've been through it, or been put through it, which ever you prefer and you need quiet, as the deaf mute said to the piano tuner. Mighty, Her Ladyship thought you were tonight, she did, that was the word she used, mighty. Of course, I cannot comment on the storm scene but I did hear, 'O Reason not the need'. Tremble-making. Never seen you so full of the real thing, if you don't mind my saying so, Sir. And wasn't Geoffrey agile as Fool? For a man of his age. Kept well down-stage, never once got in your light, much less obtrusive than Mr Davenport-Scott. In every way. And here's something funny. In the storm scene, when we were beating ourselves delirious, and I was having to jump between thunder-sheet and timpani like a juggler with rubber balls and Indian clubs, Mr Oxenby came to our aid uninvited. Cracked and clapped he did with abandon. Not a word said, just gave assistance when assistance was needed. Afterwards, just before the interval, I thanked him. "Get stuffed," he said which wasn't nice, and added scornfully, "I don't know why I helped." And I said, "Because we're a band of brothers, and you're one of us in spite of yourself." I did, that's what I said, quite unabashed. He hobbled away, head down, and if he was given to muttering, he'd have muttered. Darkly. [*Pause.*] More tea? Are you asleep, Sir?

SIR: To be driven thus. I hate the swines.

NORMAN: Who? Who is it you hate? The critics?

SIR: The critics? Hate the critics? I have nothing but compassion for them. How can one hate the crippled, the mentally deficient and the dead? Bastards.

NORMAN: Who then?

SIR: Who then what?

NORMAN: Who then what is it you hate?

SIR: Let me rest, Norman, you must stop questioning me, let me rest. But don't leave me till I'm asleep. Don't leave me alone. [*Pause.*] I am a spent force. [*Pause.*] My days are numbered.

> [*Silence.* NORMAN *watches him, then takes out his brandy bottle but finds it empty. He tiptoes out of the room. In the corridor he meets* HER LADYSHIP, *carrying a sewing-bag.*]

HER LADYSHIP: Is he asleep?

NORMAN: I think so.

HER LADYSHIP: I'll sit with him.

NORMAN: Don't wake him, will you, your ladyship. He's ever so tired.

> [*He goes.* HER LADYSHIP *enters* SIR's *dressing room and deliberately makes a noise.* SIR *starts.*]

SIR: Is it my cue?

HER LADYSHIP: No. It's still the interval.

> [*She sits and begins to darn pairs of tights.*]

I have things to say.

SIR: Norman tells me you thought I was mighty tonight.

HER LADYSHIP: I never said anything of the kind. He makes these things up.

[*Pause.*]

SIR: What have you to say?

HER LADYSHIP: What I always have to say.

SIR: You know my answer.

HER LADYSHIP: You've worked hard. You've saved. Enough's enough. Tonight, in your curtain speech, make the announcement.

SIR: I can't.

HER LADYSHIP: You won't.

SIR: I've no choice.

HER LADYSHIP: You'll die. Or end up a vegetable. Well, that's your affair. But you're not going to drag me with you.

SIR: I am helpless, Pussy. I do what I'm told. I cower, frightened of being whipped. I am driven.

HER LADYSHIP: Driven, no. Obstinate, yes, cruel, yes, ruthless, yes.

SIR: Don't.

HER LADYSHIP: For an actor you have a woeful lack of insight. Use your great imagination, use your inspired gifts, try to feel what I feel, what I'm forced to go through.

SIR: I do. But I need you beside me, familiar, real.

HER LADYSHIP: I am beside you, darning tights. Very familiar, quite real. All I ask, Bonzo, is that we stop now. Tonight. The end of the week. But no more. I can't take any more.

SIR: If it were possible—

HER LADYSHIP: It is possible—

SIR: No—

HER LADYSHIP: You deceive no one but yourself.

SIR: If that were true why then am I here, with the bombs falling, risking life and limb, why?

Not by choice. I have a duty. I have to keep faith.

HER LADYSHIP: Balls.

SIR: What?

HER LADYSHIP: You do nothing without self-interest. And you drag everyone with you. Me. Chained. Not even by law.

SIR: Would marriage have made so much difference to you?

HER LADYSHIP: You misunderstand. Deliberately.

SIR: I should have made her divorce me.

HER LADYSHIP: You didn't get a divorce because you wanted a knighthood.

SIR: Not true.

HER LADYSHIP: True. You know where your priorities lie. Whatever you do is to your advantage and to no one else's. Talk about being driven. You make yourself sound like a disinterested stage-hand. You do nothing without self-interest. Self. You. Alone.

SIR: Pussy, please, I'm sinking, don't push me further into the mud—

HER LADYSHIP: Sir. Her Ladyship. Fantasies. For God's sake, you're a third-rate actor-manager on a tatty tour of the provinces, not some Colossus bestriding the narrow world. Sir. Her Ladyship. Look at me. Darning tights. Look at you. Lear's hovel is luxury compared to this.

SIR: I'm surprised at you, Pussy. With your inheritance. Your father was of the breed. He donned the purple.

HER LADYSHIP: Donned the purple. The breed. Service. I've heard it all my life. My father also talked as if he were decreeing the apostolic succession.

SIR: I'm not well, I have half of Lear's lifetime yet to live, I have to lift you in my arms, I have howl, howl, howl yet to speak.

HER LADYSHIP: Sir. Her Ladyship. We're a laughing-stock. You'd never get a knighthood because the King doesn't possess a double-edged sword. The only honour you'll ever get is when you go on stage and we all bow.

[*Silence.*]

SIR: Do you remember, years ago, one of our Gonerils, a tall dark handsome girl with a Grecian nose—

HER LADYSHIP: Flora Bacon.

SIR: Was it, yes, perhaps it was. Flora. Do you remember the night I was rather hard on Norman because he'd got my tights inside out during the quick change in *The Wandering Jew*? Or was it *The Sign of the Cross*? Whichever. She turned on me. "He may be your servant," she said, "but he's a human being." Then, to Norman, she said, "Why don't you leave him? Why do you put up with it?" And Norman said, "Don't fuss. He only gives as good as he gets. He has to take it out on someone." He was right. These are the penalties of aspiration and ambition: single-mindedness, intolerance and unspent energy. So awful are they to bear that faith, struggle and duty must stand for them. And so awful are they to bear that others, not so cursed, must suffer in their presence. Norman understands. He knows it is not me but what is given to me, bursting out of me, passed on ruthlessly. Flora Bacon didn't understand. Slave-driver she called me. Why did I ever employ her?

HER LADYSHIP: Her mother was Lady Bacon. She invested £200 in the company.

SIR: I've given work to a good few Bolsheviks in my time. Slave-driver? Me? [*Long pause.*]

I thought tonight I caught sight of him. Or saw myself as he sees me. Speaking 'Reason not the need,' I was suddenly detached from myself. My thoughts flew. And I was observing from a great height. Go on, you bastard, I seemed to be saying or hearing. Go on, you've more to give, don't hold back more, more, more. And I was watching Lear. Each word he spoke was fresh invented. I had no knowledge of what came next, what fate awaited him. The agony was in the moment of acting created. I saw an old man and the old man was me. And I knew there was more to come. But what? Bliss, partial recovery, more pain and death. All this I knew I had yet to see. Outside myself, do you understand? Outside myself.

[*He holds out his hand. She does not take it.*] Don't leave me. I'll rest easy if you stay. Don't ask of me the impossible. Otherwise, I know, without you, in darkness, I'll see a locked door, a sign turned in the window, closed, gone away, and a drawn blind.

HER LADYSHIP: I'll stay till Norman returns.

SIR: Longer. I meant longer. Please. Please, Pussy. Reassure me. I'm sick—

HER LADYSHIP: Sick, yes, so am I. Sick. I'm sick of cold railway trains, cold waiting rooms, cold Sundays on Crewe, and cold food late at night. I'm sick of packing and unpacking and of darning tights. I'm sick of the smell of rotting costumes and naphthalene. And most of all I'm sick of reading week after week that I'm barely adequate, too old, the best of a bad supporting cast, unequal to you, unworthy of your gifts, I'm sick of having to put on a brave face. [*Pause.*] I should have

left you in Baltimore on the last American
tour. I should have accepted Mr Feldman's
offer and taken the 20th Century west.
[*Pause.*]

SIR: Feldman didn't think I'd photograph well.
Swine. I hate the cinema. I believe in living
things.

HER LADYSHIP: How quickly one's looks go.

SIR: They haven't built a camera large enough
to record me.

HER LADYSHIP: I wouldn't have minded a modest success.

SIR: Why they knighted that dwarf Arthur
Palgrove I shall never know. "Rise, Sir
Arthur," said the King, "But, Sir, I wasn't
kneeling." Not once in his whole career
did he put a toe outside London.

HER LADYSHIP: I liked America.

SIR: I hated the swines.
[*Knock on the door.*]

IRENE: [*off*] Act Two beginners, please, Sir.

SIR: I must rest now, Pussy. I want peace.

HER LADYSHIP: All you want is to have your cake and to
eat it.

SIR: I've never seen any point in having cake
unless one's going to eat it.
[*He laughs.* NORMAN *re-enters.*]

NORMAN: Everything jolly?

SIR: Don't you know what knocking is?

NORMAN: Please, Sir, not in front of Her Ladyship.
I've been mingling. You should hear what
they think out there. I've never known an
interval like it. Michaelangelo, William
Blake, God knows who else you reminded
them of. One poor boy, an airman, head
bandaged, was weeping in the stalls bar,
comforted by an older man, once blond, now
grey, parchment skin and dainty hands,

who kept on saying, "There, there, Evelyn, it's only a play," which seemed to me no comfort at all because if it wasn't a play 'There-there-Evelyn' wouldn't be so upset.

SIR: Michaelangelo, did they?

NORMAN: And Blake.

HER LADYSHIP: I'm going to my room.

SIR: Please stay.

HER LADYSHIP: You must rest, Bonzo, mustn't he, Norman?

NORMAN: Yes, he must.

SIR: Pussy—

> [*She goes.*]

Be gentle with Her Ladyship.

NORMAN: I'm always gentle with Her Ladyship.

SIR: Especially gentle.

NORMAN: Why?

SIR: Time of life.

NORMAN: You mean hot flushes and dizzy spells.

SIR: She's become very preoccupied with herself.

NORMAN: Sounds like a bad attack of change.

SIR: Be gentle. I don't want her hurt.

NORMAN: Sleep now. Is there anything else you want?

SIR: Only oblivion.

NORMAN: That'll come sooner or later and I hope later. I'll wake you in plenty of time so you can enter fantastically dressed in wild flowers. Sleep tight, don't let the fleas bite.

> [*He goes.* IRENE, *triple crown in hand, appears and watches* NORMAN *exit.* SIR *suddenly starts, rises and goes to the door, opens it and comes face to face with* IRENE.]

SIR: Fetch Madge.

> [IRENE *runs off.* SIR *finds his exercise book and, straining to see, begins to write. He makes several false starts.* MADGE *enters.* IRENE *waits outside with the triple crown.* MADGE *knocks on dressing room door and enters.*]

MADGE: Yes?

SIR: It's going well, I think.

MADGE: Except for your first entrance.

SIR: Come here.
    [*She does so.*]
    Hold my hand. Please.
    [*She takes his hand.*]

MADGE: It's like ice.

SIR: Cold with fear.

MADGE: What are you frightened of?

SIR: What's to come.

MADGE: You know who you're talking to, do you? It's me. Not someone to impress.

SIR: I'm speaking from my heart. I have never before felt so lonely.

MADGE: Please. I have a show to run—
    [*She tries to break free.*]

SIR: Listen to me. I say I'm frightened of what's to come and I mean it. Because for the first time in my life the future is hidden from me. I see no friends. I am not warmed by fellowship. I only know awful solitude.

MADGE: An occupational hazard.
    [*She breaks free.*]
    You wanted to see me. About what?

SIR: I look on you as my one true friend—

MADGE: I have to go back to the corner.

SIR: Twenty years, did you say twenty years?

MADGE: Yes.

SIR: Have you been happy? Has it been worth it?
    [*Pause.*]

MADGE: No, I've not been happy. Yes. It's been worth it.
    [*Pause.*]

SIR: Madge-dear, in my Will I've left you all my press-cutting books—

MADGE: I don't want to hear what you've left me in your Will—

SIR: Cuttings that span a lifetime, an entire career. I've kept them religiously. Good and bad notices alike. Not all that many bad. Talk of me sometimes. Speak well of me. Actors live on only in the memory of others. Speak well of me.

MADGE: This is a ridiculous conversation. You are in the middle of a performance of *Lear,* playing rather less mechanically than you have of late, and you talk as if you're organising your own memorial service.

SIR: The most wonderful thing in life is to be remembered. Speak well of me. You'll be believed.

MADGE: You'll be remembered.

[*Pause.*]

SIR: Madge-dear, I have something for you.

[*He opens a box on his dressing table and finds a ring.*]

I want you to have this ring. If possessions can be dear then this ring is the dearest thing I own. This ring was worn by Edmund Kean in a play whose title is an apt inscription for what I feel: *A New Way to Pay Old Debts.* When you talk of it, say Edmund Kean and I wore it.

[*He puts the ring into her hand. She tries not to show her feelings.*]

I once had it in mind to give it to you years ago, but you were younger then, and I thought you would misunderstand.

MADGE: Yes. A ring from a man to a woman is easily misunderstood.

SIR: I know I'm thought insensitive, but I'm not blind.

MADGE: No. I've always known you were aware of what the spinster in the corner felt. [*Pause.*]

You were right not to give me a ring years ago. I lived in hope then. [*Pause.*] At least I've seen you every day, made myself useful to you. I settled for what I could get. I was always aware of my limitations.

SIR: You are the only one who really, truly, loves me.

> [*She gives him back the ring and goes quickly from the room. He puts the ring on. He turns back to his exercise book and continues to write.* IRENE *knocks gently on the door.*]

Who?

IRENE: Irene. I'm returning the triple crown, Sir.

SIR: Come.

> [*She enters the room.*]

Put it down.

> [*She does so. He continues to write. Pause.*]

IRENE: Sir, will it disturb you if I say something?

SIR: It depends on what it is.

IRENE: I just wanted to thank you.

SIR: For what?

IRENE: The performance this evening.

SIR: It's not over yet.

IRENE: I felt honoured to be on the stage.

> [*Pause.*]

SIR: Open that drawer you will find a photograph of me.

> [*She does so. He inscribes it.*]

IRENE: I love coming into this room. I can feel the power. And the mystery. In days gone by this would have been the place where the High Priests robed. I feel frightened. As though I'm trespassing.

SIR: A kindred spirit.

> [*They look at each other.*]

Lock the door.

> [*She does so.*]

Come nearer—

IRENE: Irene.

SIR: Irene. And you want to act.

IRENE: Yes.

SIR: Passionately?

IRENE: Yes.

SIR: With every fibre of your being?

IRENE: Yes.

SIR: To the exclusion of all else?

IRENE: Yes.

SIR: You must be prepared to sacrifice what most people call life.

IRENE: I am.

[*Long pause.*]

SIR: Your birth sign?

IRENE: Scorpio.

[*In the corridor* NORMAN *enters, comes to the door, tries it gently but finds it locked. He listens at the key-hole.*]

SIR: Good. Ambition, secretiveness, loyalty and capable of great jealousy. Essential qualities for the theatre. Have you good legs?

[*She shrugs.*]

SIR: Come closer. Let me see.

[*She raises her skirt.*]

Higher.

[*She does so.*]

Too good. All the best actresses have legs like tree-trunks.

[*He feels her thighs.*]

There's not much to you.

[*He feels her hips.*]

Such small bones.

[*His hands wander up to her breasts.*]

Are you getting enough to eat?

[*He takes her face in his hands and seems about to kiss her.*]

So young, so young.
> [*Suddenly, in one movement he lifts her bodily into his arms. She cries out.*]

[*a great roar*] That's more like it!
> [*He staggers, lowers her to the ground, then waves her away.*]

Too late, too late.
> [*She runs to the door, unlocks it, goes into the corridor and comes face to face with* NORMAN, *who grabs her by the wrist.* NORMAN *shuts the door.* SIR *sits, scribbles, then rests.*]

NORMAN: Well now, my dainty duck, my dear-o.

IRENE: Let go of me.

NORMAN: What was all that about?
> [*Pause.*]

IRENE: He seems better.

NORMAN: Better than what or whom as the case may be?

IRENE: I didn't think he'd get through the performance tonight.

NORMAN: He's not through it yet. [*Pause.*] I'm waiting.

IRENE: For what?

NORMAN: A graphic description of events. Out with it. Or I shall slap your face. Hard. You had better know that my parentage is questionable, and that I can be vicious when roused.

IRENE: I thought we were friends.

NORMAN: I thought so, too, Irene. I shall long remember welcoming you into the company in the prop room of the Palace Theatre, Newark-on-Trent, the smell of size and carpenter's glue, the creaking of skips and you locked in the arms of the Prince of Morocco, a married man, ever such a comic sight with his tights round his ankles and you smeared black. I said, "Don't worry, mum's the word, but don't let it happen again." We talked, brewed tea on a paint-stained gas-ring, under a photograph of Mr Charles Doran as Shylock, somewhat askew and ever so disapproving. You expressed gratitude and I said, "Now you're one of the family." And this is how you repay me.

IRENE: What am I supposed to have done?

NORMAN: You tell me.

IRENE: About what?

NORMAN: About Sir, the Guv'nor, the Chief, Father, Him from whom all favours flow. You know who Sir is, Irene.

IRENE: I'm late. I have to help Her Ladyship with her armour.

NORMAN: Her Ladyship's armour will keep. Perhaps you didn't hear my question. What did Sir do?

IRENE: I'm not telling you—

[*He grabs her closer and threatens to strike her.*]

NORMAN: I'll mark you for life, ducky.

IRENE: You strike me and I'll tell him, I'll tell Sir, I'll tell Sir, I will, I'll tell Sir—

[*He lets go of her.*]

NORMAN: Tell Sir? On me? I quake in my boots. I shan't be able to eat my tea. Tell Sir? Gadzooks, madam, the thought of it, you telling Sir on me. Ducky, in his present state, which totters between confusion and chaos, to tell Sir anything at all would take a louder voice and clearer diction than that possessed by the most junior member of this Shakespearean troupe, the assistant stage-manager, dog's body, general understudy, map-carrier and company mattress, namely you. You won't be able to tell Sir you'd let him touch your tits on a Thursday matinee in Aberystwyth. Tell Sir. You think I don't know the game? You think I've dressed the rotten bugger for sixteen bloody years, nursed him, spoiled him, washed his sweat-sodden doublet and hose and his foul underpants night after night without knowing every twist and turn of what is laughingly known as his mind? Never mind tell Sir. I'll tell you. He did something, something unseen and furtive, something that gave him pleasure. "That's more like it!" More like what, Irene? I have to know all that occurs. I have to know all he does.

    [*Pause.*]

IRENE: He lifted me up in his arms.

NORMAN: Lifted you up?

IRENE: And I understood, I understood what he meant. "So young, so young," he said, and lifted me up. "That's more like it," he cried and I knew, cradled in his arms, that it was youth and newness he was after—

    [NORMAN *laughs.*]

—why do you laugh? I was there, it happened, it's true, I felt it. He was trembling and so was I. Up in his arms, part of him, "that's more like it", and he lowered me, waved me away and I ran off. Youth. And with my eyes closed I imagined what it would be like to be carried on by him, Cordelia, dead in his arms, young.

NORMAN: Never mind a young Cordelia, ducky, he wants a light Cordelia. Light, ducky, light. Look at yourself. Look at Her Ladyship.

IRENE: You don't understand. He needs youth—

NORMAN: Ducky, we tried *The Master Builder* in Leamington Spa. Three performances.

We played to absolutely no business at all
so don't give me all that wish-wash about
youth, I know all about youth knocking at
the door, ducky, and audiences stay away in
droves, me included. "That's more like it."
You're lighter than she is, ducky. [*He laughs.
Pause.*] You're not the first to be placed on
the scales. How do you think Her Ladyship
got the job? Her Ladyship, when a slip of a
girl, went from map-carrier to youngest
daughter overnight. I remember it well.
That was the tour the Doge of Venice gave
Lancelot Gobbo clap.

> [IRENE *begins to cry softly.*]

It's not youth or talent or star quality he's
after, ducky, but a moderate eater. [*Pause.*]
We could cope with anything in those days.
Turmoil was his middle name.

> [NORMAN *sways a little, then controls himself.
> He becomes tearful but holds back.*]

So. Ducky. Keep well away. The old days
are gone, the days of vim and vigour, what's
to come is still unsure. Trip no further,
pretty sweeting. We can't have any distrac-
tions. Not anymore. Not if things are to be
lovely. And painless. [*Pause.*] Don't disobey
me, will you? The fateful words, "You finish
on Saturday" have a decidedly sinister ring—

> [HER LADYSHIP *appears.*]

—two rings, and bangles right up to the
elbow.

HER LADYSHIP: There you are. You're late with my armour.
[*She goes.*]

NORMAN: Off you go, ducky. You have to find another
.canoe to paddle. Ours, I'm afraid, has holes.

> [IRENE *goes.* NORMAN *swigs from his brandy
> bottle. He goes into* SIR's *dressing room.
> Gently, he shakes* SIR *awake.*]

Fantastically dressed in wild flowers.

> [SIR *rises. In silence* NORMAN *helps him to change costumes and then bedecks him in wild flowers.*]

SIR: Michaelangelo, did they?

NORMAN: And Blake.

SIR: I knew what they mean. Moral grandeur.

> [*Pause.*]

NORMAN: I talked to the girl. She's not as light as she looks. We're none of us strong enough for a change of cast.

> [*Pause.* SIR, *suddenly and fiercely, embraces* NORMAN.]

SIR: You cannot be properly paid. *In pectora,* I name you friend. The debt is all mine. And I shall find a way to repay you. I must, must settle all my debts.

NORMAN: Don't, you're making me tearful—

SIR: [*letting go of him*] God, your breath smells of stale tights. How much have you had?

NORMAN: Not enough.

SIR: Iago, Iago—

NORMAN: Wrong play.

SIR: I have to wake in bliss, I have to carry on Her Ladyship, I need you sober.

NORMAN: I am. Sober. Diction perfect. Deportment steady. Temper serene.

> [NORMAN *smiles.*]

SIR: It is no laughing matter! [*Pause.*] The final push. I hope you're up to it.

NORMAN: [*under his breath*] And you, dear.

SIR: What?

NORMAN: And you, Lear.

> [*They begin to go.*]

> [*Lights fade to blackout.*]

> [*Drums. Trumpets. Clash of swords. Light grows.*]

[*The wings.* SIR, HER LADYSHIP *and* NORMAN *stand in readiness,* IRENE *by the timpani.*]

[SIR *spits on his hands.*]

HER LADYSHIP: I wish you wouldn't do that. You remind me of a labourer.

[SIR *lifts* HER LADYSHIP *in his arms and carries her on. Those in the wings watch.*]

[*Lights fade to blackout.*]

[*Lights up again quickly.*]

[IRENE *drums a slow, sombre rhythm.*]

MADGE: Cue curtain down.

KENT

I am come
To bid my King and master aye good-night;
Is he not here?

ALBANY

Speak, Edmund, where's the King?...

EDMUND

I pant for life; some good I mean to do
Despite of mine own nature. Quickly send,
Be brief in it, to the castle; for my writ
Is on the life of Lear and on Cordelia.
Nay, send in time.

ALBANY

Run, run! O run!...
Haste thee, for thy life.

SIR

Howl, howl, howl, howl! O! you are men of stones:
Had I your tongues and eyes, I'd use them so
That heaven's vaults should crack. She's gone for ever.
I know when one is dead, and when one lives;
She's dead as earth...

KENT

Break, heart; I prithee, break.

ALBANY

The weight of this sad time we must obey;
Speak what we feel, not what we ought to say.
The oldest hath borne most: we that are young,
Shall never see so much, nor live so long.

[*Sound of curtain falling. Applause.* SIR *comes into the wings.*]

SIR: [*looking heavenwards*] We've done it Will, we've done it.

MADGE: Stand by for curtain-calls. Curtain going up.

[*The company take their curtain calls.*]

Stand by for your curtain-call, Sir.

[SIR *goes on for his call. Thunderous applause and cheers.*]

[*Lights change to a solitary light, bright and harsh.* SIR *steps into the light and* NORMAN *stands just behind him in shadow. Applause and cheers continue until* SIR *raises his hand for silence.*]

SIR: My lords, ladies and gentlemen. Thank you for the manner in which you have received the greatest tragedy in our language. We live in dangerous times. Our civilisation is under threat from the forces of darkness, and we, humble actors, do all in our power to fight as soldiers on the side of right in the great battle. Our most cherished ambition is to keep the best alive of our drama, to serve the greatest poet-dramatist who has ever lived, and we are animated by nothing else than to educate the nation in his works by taking his plays to every corner of our beloved island. Tomorrow night we shall give—

NORMAN: *Richard III.*

SIR: —*King Richard III.* I myself will play the hunchback king. On Saturday afternoon my lady wife will play—

NORMAN: Portia.

SIR: —Portia, and I the badly-wronged Jew in *The Merchant of Venice*, a play you may think of greater topicality than ever. On Saturday night—

NORMAN: *Lear.*

SIR: —On Saturday night we shall essay once more the tragedy you have this evening witnessed and I myself shall again undergo the severest test known to an actor. Next week, God willing, we shall be in—

NORMAN: Eastbourne.

SIR: —Eastbourne. I trust your friends and relatives there will, on your kind recommendation, discover source for refreshment, as you seem to have done by your warm indication, in the glorious words we are privileged to speak. For the generous manner in which you have received our earnest endeavours, on behalf of my lady wife, my company and myself, I remain your humble and obedient servant, and can no other answer make but thanks and thanks, and ever thanks.

[*Bows. Applause. He steps out of the light. Applause continues.*]

[*Light fades.*]

[*Light on* SIR's *dressing room and corridor.*]

[SIR *is seated at the dressing table with Scotch and beer.* NORMAN *puts the costume away and starts to clean the moustache and beard which* SIR *has removed.* SIR *downs the Scotch in one, and sips the beer.*]

SIR: Norman, Norman—

NORMAN: Sir?

SIR: What will happen to you?

NORMAN: Could you be a little more explicit?

SIR: What will happen to you if I can't continue?

NORMAN: Stop it. Nothing ever happens to me. I lead a life quite without incident.

SIR: But if I should be unable to continue.

NORMAN: There's no chance of that so I'm not bothering to answer.

SIR: I worry about you, my boy.

NORMAN: Don't.

SIR: You could become a steward on a ship.

NORMAN: What and give up the theatre?

SIR: I know several ship-owners. They'd help.

NORMAN: I'll trouble you not to trouble them or yourself.

SIR: What will you do?

NORMAN: As best I can.

[*Pause.*]

SIR: What is the play tomorrow?

NORMAN: *Richard III*.

SIR: Again? Who planned this tour?

NORMAN: You did.

SIR: Slavery, bloody slavery.

[*Knock on the door.*]

NORMAN: Who?

GEOFFREY: Geoffrey.

SIR: Come.

[GEOFFREY *enters, dressed in street clothes.*]

GEOFFREY: Just popped in to say goodnight, old man.

SIR: Goodnight, Geoffrey. Very fine in the storm scene, my boy. Felt your love, that's what matters.

GEOFFREY: Thank you. Fool is by far the most important part I've ever played in Shakespeare. I hope I didn't let you down.

SIR: Offer Geoffrey a small glass of beer, Norman.

GEOFFREY: Thank you.

[NORMAN *pours a small glass of beer and gives it to* GEOFFREY.]

Such an odd feeling tonight, old man, rather exciting to reach my age to prove to others that one can act. That's the wonderful thing about this life of ours. It's never too late. Surprising things happen. But there are disadvantages. One gets the taste for more. Cheers.

SIR: Good health attend you.

NORMAN: Bottoms up, Geoffrey.

GEOFFREY: May I ask you a question, old man?

SIR: Ask.

GEOFFREY: Fool is a curious role. You give your all for almost an hour and a half, then vanish into thin air for the rest of the play. The next one hears of me is you saying that I'm hanged. But why? By whom? It seems awfully unfair.

SIR: My theory is that, in William's day, Fool and Cordelia were played by one and the same person. Must've been a good double, Fool and Cordelia. Saved a salary, too, of course.

GEOFFREY: Well. Things haven't changed. As long as you feel I didn't let you down.

SIR: In no particular.

GEOFFREY: Just one last thing, I won't keep you, I know you're very tired. But when you interviewed me, I said I didn't want too much. Small parts, I said. It may not be thought admirable but I've never put a jot at risk. Never wanted to scale the heights. Played goodish parts, tours of course, never London. I don't complain. Touring's a good life. Enjoyed my cricket in summer, hockey in winter, lovely women, long walks, a weekly change of scene, the English countryside in all weathers. What could be nicer? But never risked a jot. Been lucky. Mustn't complain. I expect I can get through to the end of the chapter. I've a little put by. My wife brings in a bit with her singing lessons. I've no right to expect work, not at my age. War's brought surprising employment. All the youngsters at front. My grandson, not a pro, was taken prisoner in Tripoli. Sorry to be so long-winded. Point is, if at any time circumstances arise, I should like to be considered for better parts. I shouldn't want an increase in salary.

SIR: I will keep you in the forefront of my mind.

GEOFFREY: Thank you, old man. Well. Goodnight. Thank you for the drink.

> [GEOFFREY *stumbles.* NORMAN *moves to help him.*]

I can manage.

> [GEOFFREY *exits.*]

SIR: Fine fellow. Fine fellow.

NORMAN: Shouldn't we remove our make-up, Sir?

> [SIR *stares at himself in the looking-glass.*]

SIR: I hope Will's pleased tonight.

NORMAN: I had a friend—

SIR: Not now, Norman—

NORMAN: I had a friend had ever such a sweet singing voice but lost it in Colwyn Bay after a bad attack of sea mist. But it came back to him in the end, and d'you know why? Because he said to himself they also sing who only stand and serve. Or words to that effect.

SIR: Are you pissed, Norman?

NORMAN: Me, Sir? Pissed, Sir? Lud, Sir Percy, how you do tousle me.

SIR: Let me smell your breath.

> [NORMAN *gives a short puff of breath away from* SIR.]

NORMAN: There. Told you. Sweeter than Winston Churchill.

SIR: I can't have you pissed.

> [HER LADYSHIP *enters dressed in her own clothes.*]

HER LADYSHIP: Not changed yet?

SIR: I've been a little slow tonight, Pussy.

HER LADYSHIP: I'm not waiting. I'll go back to the digs, see if I can get a fire lit.

SIR: I shan't be long.

HER LADYSHIP: Goodnight, Norman. I'm not certain whether I should thank you or not.

NORMAN: Not. I can't bear being thanked.

[*She goes.*]

SIR: A good woman.

[SIR *applies cold cream slowly and wearily.* OXENBY *knocks on the door.*]

Who?

OXENBY: Mr Oxenby.

[SIR *makes a gesture to imply he doesn't want to see him.* NORMAN *opens the door.*]

NORMAN: What do you want?

OXENBY: My manuscript. He won't read it, I know that.

NORMAN: Keep your voice down. He hasn't gone yet. Wait there. He's a little slow tonight.

[NORMAN *begins to look for* OXENBY'S *manuscript.* OXENBY *waits in the doorway.*]

OXENBY: [*deliberately loud*] All that struggling and surviving has tired him, no doubt.

[NORMAN *darts back to the door.*]

NORMAN: Please, Mr Oxenby.

OXENBY: [*hissing*] Outmoded hypocrite.

SIR: What—what—?

NORMAN: Not now, Mr Oxenby.

OXENBY: Death to all tyrants.

SIR: What, what did he say?

[NORMAN *finds the play and gives it to* OXENBY.]

OXENBY: Tell him from me, I look forward to a new order. I want a company without tyrants.

NORMAN: Who'd be in charge?

OXENBY: I would.

[*He smiles.*]

NORMAN: Don't write him off. Or me. Or Her Ladyship. She has a very fine pedigree. Her father—

OXENBY: I saw her father. As Caliban. A good make-up artist, that's all.

SIR: Close that door.

NORMAN: You'll be lovely with a little success, Mr Oxenby.

OXENBY: Your nose is browner than usual tonight, Norman.

[*He goes.*]

NORMAN: The little you know—

SIR: What did Oxenby want?

[IRENE *enters the corridor and pauses at* SIR's *door.*]

IRENE: Goodnight, Sir. Goodnight, Norman.

NORMAN: If you hurry, you'll catch Mr Oxenby.

[*She goes.* SIR *begins to smear the cold cream and when the mask is covered and the colours a blur, he lets out a sudden moan and cannot apparently move.*]

NORMAN: Sir, what is it, Sir?

[SIR *moans.*]

SIR: I'm—I'm tired. Terribly tired. The room is spinning. I—I must lie down.

[NORMAN *quickly helps him to the couch.* SIR *lies back.*]

See if you can get me a taxi in this God-forsaken place.

NORMAN: All in good time.

[*No response.* NORMAN *takes cotton wool and begins to clean* SIR's *face.* SIR *begins to cry.*]

Don't cry. Don't cry.

SIR: There's nothing left.

NORMAN: Stop that at once. I had a friend—

SIR: Oh for Christ's sake, I'm sick of your friends.

Motley crew they are. Pathetic, lonely, despairing—

NORMAN: That's nice, isn't it.

[*Pause.*]

SIR: I beg your pardon. Uncalled for. Count myself as your friend.

NORMAN: Never despairing.

SIR: Have apologised.

NORMAN: Never, never despairing. Well. Perhaps. Sometimes. At night. Or at Christmas when you can't get a panto. But not once inside the building. Never. Pathetic maybe, but not ungrateful. Too mindful of one's luck, as the saying goes. No Duke is more privileged. Here's beauty. Here's spring and summer. Here pain is bearable. And never lonely. Not here. For he today that sheds his blood with me. Soft, no doubt. Sensitive. That's my nature. Easily hurt, but that's a virtue. I'm not here for reasons of my own either. No one could accuse me of base motives. I've got what I want and I don't need anyone to know it. Inadequate, yes. But never, never despairing.

SIR: I've begun *My Life*.

NORMAN: What?

SIR: Fetch it. The book. I made a start—

[NORMAN *brings it to him.*]

Find the place.

[NORMAN *pages through the book.*]

NORMAN: You didn't get very far—

SIR: What did I write?

NORMAN: [*He reads:*] My Life. Dedication. This book is dedicated to My Beloved Pussy who has been my splendid spur. To the spirit of all actors because of their faith and endurance which never fails them. To Those who do the work of the theatre yet have but small share in its glory: Carpenters, Electricians. Scene-shifters, Property men. To the Audiences, who have laughed with us, have wept with us and whose hearts have united with ours in sympathy and understanding. And Finally— ah Sir—to the memory of William Shakespeare in whose glorious service we all labour.

[*Silence.*]

SIR: *My Life* will have to do.

[*Silence.*]

NORMAN: Wait a moment, wait a moment—

[*He re-reads the passage.*]

"Carpenters, electricians, property-men..." But Sir, Sir—

[NORMAN *looks at him.*]

Sir? Sir?

[*He shakes* SIR *gently. A long pause.*]

We're not dead are we?

[*Silence.*]

That's your cue. You know the line. "You lie! Jack Clinton—"

[*He pretends to tear off a moustache. Silence.*]

—lives!" Talk about untoward.

[*For the first time* NORMAN's *drunkenness shows physically. He staggers, almost falls—*]

You're right. The room is spinning.

[*He regains his balance, stands staring at* SIR, *then is seized by terror and panic. He stumbles to the door—*]

Your ladyship! Madge! Anybody!

[*He stands in the doorway, whimpering.* MADGE *hurries into the corridor, then past him into the dressing room.* NORMAN *takes a step inside and watches her.* MADGE *looks down at* SIR. *She is perfectly still. She lets out a soft, short cry but then controls herself. Silence.*]

Wasn't much of a death scene. Unremarkable and ever so short. For him.

[MADGE *turns away from the body.*]

MADGE: Where's Her Ladyship?

NORMAN: Left before he did. Couldn't wait.

MADGE: I'll telephone her. And I'll get a doctor.

NORMAN: Too late for a doctor, ducky.

[MADGE *leaves the room. As she passes* NORMAN—]

What's to happen to me?

MADGE: Close the door. Wait outside.

NORMAN: I don't want to wait outside. I never wait outside. I want to be with him. I know my place.

MADGE: Try and sober up.

[*She goes.* NORMAN, *half-afraid, goes tentatively into the room. He cannot look at the body. He goes straight to the exercise book and opens it. He reads to himself.*]

NORMAN: "Carpenters, electricians, property men?" Cruel bastard. You might have remembered.

[*Silence.* NORMAN *looks about to make sure he is unobserved. He finds a pencil and writes in the exercise book. Then, like an angry child, he turns on* SIR's *body and thumbs his nose at it violently. But he begins to whimper again. He drinks brandy from* SIR's *drinks tray.* MADGE *returns.*]

MADGE: Her Ladyship's coming at once. She took it very calmly. She asked for him to be covered in his Lear cloak. Where is it?

NORMAN: Covered in his Lear cloak? Fetch the photographer, ducky. Covered in his Lear cloak? This isn't the Death of Nelson, you know.

MADGE: Where is it?

[*He points. She gets the cloak.* NORMAN *looks away. She is about to cover* SIR *but first surreptitiously slips the ring off his finger and pockets it. Then she covers him.* NORMAN *suddenly laughs.*]

NORMAN: There's no mention of stage managers, either.

MADGE: Come out of here.

NORMAN: Are we going to get paid? I mean, is there money in the till after deductions for income tax? We've got to be paid the full week, you know. Just because the man dies on a Thursday doesn't mean we should get paid *pro rata*.

MADGE: Wait outside.

NORMAN: You're nothing now, ducky. He took away your stripes. And mine. How could he be so bloody careless?

MADGE: Come away.

NORMAN: And then where will I go? Where? I'm nowhere out of my element. I don't want to end up running a boarding house in West-cliffe-on-Sea. Or Colwyn Bay. What am I going to do?

MADGE: You can speak well of him.

NORMAN: Speak well of that old sod? I wouldn't give him a good character, not in a court of law. Ungrateful bastard. Silence, ducky. My lips are sealed.

MADGE: Get out. I don't want you in here.

NORMAN: Holy, holy, holy, is it? Are we in a shrine? No pissing on the altar—

MADGE: Stop it.

NORMAN: He never once took me out for a meal. Never once. Always a back seat, me. Can't even remember him buying me a drink. And just walks out, leaves me, no thought for anyone but himself. What have I been doing here all these years? Why? Yes, well, reason not the

need, rotten bugger. Beg your pardon, leave
the room, turn round three times and come
back—come back—

[*He breaks off and turns away from her.*]

Speak well of him? I know what you'd say,
ducky. I know all about you. I've got eyes in
my head. We all have our little sorrows.

[MADGE *goes but* NORMAN *does not notice.*]

I know what you'd say, stiff upper, faithful,
loyal. Loving. Well, I have only one thing to
say about him and I wouldn't say it in front
of you—or Her Ladyship, or anyone. Lips
tight shut. I wouldn't give you the pleasure.
Or him. Specially not him. If I said what I
have to say he'd find a way to take it out on
me. No one will ever know. We all have our
little sorrows, ducky, you're not the only
one. The littler you are, the larger the
sorrow. You think *you* loved him? What
about me?

[*Long silence.*]

This is not a place for death. I had a friend—

[*He turns suddenly as if aware of someone
behind him, but realises he is alone.*]

Sir? Sir?

[*Silence. He hugs the exercise book. He
sings—*]

"He that has and a little tiny wit,
With hey, ho, the wind and the rain."

[*He falls silent.*]

[*He stares into space.*]

[*Lights fade.*]

THE END

OTHER GROVE PRESS DRAMA AND THEATER PAPERBACKS